Workbook

Science

PEARSON
Scott
Foresman

Editorial Offices: Glenview, Illinois • Parsippany, New Jersey • New York, New York
Sales Offices: Needham, Massachusetts • Duluth, Georgia • Glenview, Illinois
Coppell, Texas • Sacramento, California • Mesa, Arizona

www.sfsuccessnet.com

Series Authors

Dr. Timothy Cooney

Professor of Earth Science and Science Education
University of Northern Iowa (UNI)
Cedar Falls, Iowa

Dr. Jim Cummins

Professor
Department of Curriculum,
Teaching, and Learning
The University of Toronto
Toronto, Canada

Dr. James Flood

Distinguished Professor of Literacy and Language
School of Teacher Education
San Diego State University
San Diego, California

Barbara Kay Foots, M.Ed.

Science Education Consultant
Houston, Texas

Dr. M. Jenice Goldston

Associate Professor of Science Education
Department of Elementary Education
Programs
University of Alabama
Tuscaloosa, Alabama

Dr. Shirley Gholston Key

Associate Professor of Science Education
Instruction and Curriculum Leadership
Department
College of Education
University of Memphis
Memphis, Tennessee

Dr. Diane Lapp

Distinguished Professor of Reading and Language Arts in Teacher Education
San Diego State University
San Diego, California

Sheryl A. Mercier

Classroom Teacher
Dunlap Elementary School
Dunlap, California

Dr. Karen L. Ostlund

UTeach, College of Natural Sciences
The University of Texas at Austin
Austin, Texas

Dr. Nancy Romance

Professor of Science Education & Principal Investigator
NSF/IERI Science IDEAS Project
Charles E. Schmidt College
of Science
Florida Atlantic University
Boca Raton, Florida

Dr. William Tate

Chair and Professor of Education and Applied Statistics
Department of Education
Washington University
St. Louis, Missouri

Dr. Kathryn C. Thornton

Professor
School of Engineering and
Applied Science
University of Virginia
Charlottesville, Virginia

Dr. Leon Ukens

Professor of Science Education
Department of Physics, Astronomy,
and Geosciences
Towson University
Towson, Maryland

Steve Weinberg

Consultant
Connecticut Center for
Advanced Technology
East Hartford, Connecticut

Consulting Author

Dr. Michael P. Klentschy

Superintendent
El Centro Elementary School District
El Centro, California

Unit A
Life Science

Unit B
Earth Science

Unit C
Physical Science

Unit D
Space and Technology

Elapsed Time

Jim will take care of the garden in July. The plants in the garden need to be watered every three days. They need to be weeded every seven days.

July						
				1 Weed Water	2	3
4	5	6	7	8	9	10
11	12	13	14	15	16	17
18	19	20	21	22	23	24
25	26	27	28	29	30	31

1. Jim weeds and waters the garden on July 1. Circle the days in July when he needs to water. Put a star next to the days when he needs to weed.

2. On what dates will Jim weed the garden?

   _____

3. On what dates will Jim water the garden?

   _____

4. How many more times will Jim water the garden than weed it?

   _____

Notes for Home: Your child learned how to measure elapsed time in a process. **Home Activity:** Discuss ways your child could have figured out the dates for the calendar. (by counting off days or by adding 3 and 7, respectively, to the date over and over)

Notes

Choose a word to complete each sentence. Underline clues that helped you decide.

vertebrate	inherited	hibernate	pupa
adaptations	migrate	larva	traits

1. A dog, a fish, and a person are all examples of a _____, or an animal with a backbone.

2. An insect egg may hatch into a _____, which eats a lot and grows fast.

3. _____, such as sharp teeth or webbed feet, help an animal survive where it lives.

4. _____ are body features passed on by an animal to its young.

5. A trait that is always passed on from parents to offspring is said to be _____.

6. A caterpillar forms a hard shell around itself and becomes a _____. When it comes out, it will be an adult.

7. Some animals _____ to the south for the winter. There they can find food.

8. Other animals know when to _____, or slow down their bodies and sleep a long time.

Notes for Home: Your child learned the vocabulary terms for Chapter 2.
Home Activity: Have your child use pictures in the text to provide examples that help define the vocabulary words. Action words can be acted out.

TARGET SKILL **Sequence**

Read the paragraph.

Kangaroo

The mother kangaroo gives birth to a tiny baby. It is only about one inch long. As soon as it is born, the baby crawls into its mother's pouch. Once there, it feeds on milk for six to eight months. Finally, it is big enough and strong enough to hop around and eat on its own.

Apply It!

What are the sequence of events in the paragraph about the kangaroo? Fill in the graphic organizer to show the correct order.

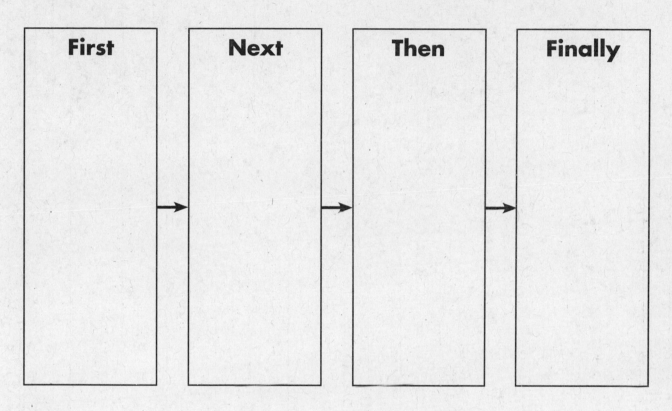

| First | Next | Then | Finally |

Notes for Home: Your child learned how to recognize the sequence of events in a process.
Home Activity: Read a library book with your child about how one animal grows and changes. Talk about the stages in the animal's life, using the words *first*, *next*, *then*, and *finally*.

Notes

Lesson 1: How are animals grouped?

Before You Read Lesson 1

Read each statement below. Place a check mark in the circle to indicate whether you agree or disagree with the statement.

	Agree	Disagree
1. There are many more invertebrates than vertebrates.	○	○
2. All vertebrates have a backbone.	○	○
3. Cats are vertebrates, but fish are not.	○	○

After You Read Lesson 1

Reread each statement above. If the lesson supports your choice, place a check mark in the *Correct* circle. Then explain how the text supports your choice. If the lesson does not support your choice, place a check mark in the *Incorrect* circle. Then explain why your choice is wrong.

	Correct	Incorrect
1. _____	○	○
_____		
2. _____	○	○
_____		
3. _____	○	○
_____		

Notes for Home: Your child has completed a pre/post inventory of key concepts in the lesson.
Home Activity: Have your child cut out magazine pictures of animals and group them to show various ways they are similar.

Reviewing Terms: Sentence Completion

Complete the sentence with the correct word or phrase.

_____ 1. _____ are features of animals, like fish's gills or scales. (Traits, Needs)

_____ 2. _____ Cats and dogs are because they have backbones. (vertebrates, invertebrates)

Reviewing Concepts: Matching

Match each vertebrate with the correct group. Write the letter on the line next to each vertebrate.

_____ 3. snake

_____ 4. frog

_____ 5. dog

a. mammal

b. reptile

c. amphibian

Match each invertebrate with the correct group. Write the letter on the line next to each invertebrate.

_____ 6. octopus

_____ 7. crab

_____ 8. earthworm

a. arthropod

b. worm

c. mollusk

Applying Strategies: Calculating

9. On a visit to the zoo, Jennifer's class saw 20 species of fishes, 5 species of amphibians, 10 species of birds, and 12 species of mammals. How many species did they see altogether? Show your work. (2 points)

_____

_____

Lesson 2: How do animals grow and change?

Before You Read Lesson 2

Read each statement below. Place a check mark in the circle to indicate whether you agree or disagree with the statement.

	Agree	Disagree
1. All animals develop inside their mothers.	○	○
2. A butterfly's first stage of life is the pupa.	○	○
3. A very young frog acts much like a fish.	○	○

After You Read Lesson 2

Reread each statement above. If the lesson supports your choice, place a check mark in the *Correct* circle. Then explain how the text supports your choice. If the lesson does not support your choice, place a check mark in the *Incorrect* circle. Then explain why your choice is wrong.

	Correct	Incorrect
1. _____	○	○
_____		
2. _____	○	○
_____		
3. _____	○	○
_____		

Notes for Home: Your child has completed a pre/post inventory of key concepts in the lesson.
Home Activity: Have your child compare photographs of himself or herself at different ages and note how he or she has changed while growing.

Reviewing Terms: Matching

Match each definition with the correct word. Write the letter on the line next to each definition.

_____ 1. the first stage of a butterfly's life cycle after hatching from an egg

_____ 2. the stage of a butterfly's life cycle when it is covered by a hard coating

a. larva
b. pupa

Reviewing Concepts: True or False

Write **T** (True) or **F** (False) on the line before each statement.

_____ 3. All animals have the same steps in their life cycles.

_____ 4. Some animals start their lives as eggs.

_____ 5. Development is the part of an animal's life cycle when it changes into an adult.

_____ 6. An adult butterfly comes out of a larva.

_____ 7. Mammals have more changes in their life cycle than insects or amphibians.

_____ 8. When mammals are born, they drink milk from their mother.

Writing

Use complete sentences to answer question 9. (2 points)

9. Describe one similarity between a butterfly's life cycle and a frog's life cycle. Describe one difference between them.

_____

_____

_____

Lesson 3: How do adaptations help animals?

Before You Read Lesson 3

Read each statement below. Place a check mark in the circle to indicate whether you agree or disagree with the statement.

	Agree	Disagree
1. Body parts are adaptations.	○	○
2. Adaptations must be learned.	○	○
3. When animals migrate, they sleep a long time.	○	○

After You Read Lesson 3

Reread each statement above. If the lesson supports your choice, place a check mark in the *Correct* circle. Then explain how the text supports your choice. If the lesson does not support your choice, place a check mark in the *Incorrect* circle. Then explain why your choice is wrong.

	Correct	Incorrect
1. _____ _____	○	○
2. _____ _____	○	○
3. _____ _____	○	○

Notes for Home: Your child has completed a pre/post inventory of key concepts in the lesson.
Home Activity: Discuss with your child some adaptations a pet (or a wild animal you can observe) has that help it survive.

Reviewing Terms: Matching

Match each definition with the correct word. Write the letter on the line next to each description.

_____ 1. a trait that helps animals meet their needs

_____ 2. when a trait is passed on from parents to their young

_____ 3. when animals move as the seasons change

_____ 4. when an animal's body systems slow down to save energy

a. inherited
b. adaptation
c. migrate
d. hibernate

Reviewing Concepts: True or False

Write **T** (True) or **F** (False) on the line before each statement.

_____ 5. A bird's bill is an adaptation that helps it meet its need for food.

_____ 6. When a harmless animal looks like a poisonous one, it is called camouflage.

_____ 7. An adaptation that allows an animal to blend in with its environment is mimicry.

_____ 8. An instinct is a behavior that an animal is born knowing how to do.

Writing

Use complete sentences to answer question 9. (2 points)

9. Describe two ways that migrating helps animals survive.

_____

_____

Lesson 4: How are animals from the past like today's animals?

Before You Read Lesson 4

Read each statement below. Place a check mark in the circle to indicate whether you agree or disagree with the statement.

	Agree	Disagree
1. A fossil is an animal skeleton.	○	○
2. Fossils show how life on Earth has changed.	○	○
3. Today's desert may have once been a jungle.	○	○

After You Read Lesson 4

Reread each statement above. If the lesson supports your choice, place a check mark in the *Correct* circle. Then explain how the text supports your choice. If the lesson does not support your choice, place a check mark in the *Incorrect* circle. Then explain why your choice is wrong.

	Correct	Incorrect
1. _____	○	○
_____		
2. _____	○	○
_____		
3. _____	○	○
_____		

Notes for Home: Your child has completed a pre/post inventory of key concepts in the lesson.
Home Activity: Have your child use modeling clay to create molds of animal parts, such as a paw or a shell. Talk about how fossils form in nature.

Reviewing Concepts: Sentence Completion

Complete each sentence with the correct word or phrase.

_____ 1. A(n) _____ is a sign of past life. (fossil, extinct)

_____ 2. Only the _____ parts of an animal become a fossil. (hard, soft)

_____ 3. A(n) _____ is formed when rock materials fill a fossil mold. (cast, amber)

_____ 4. Hardened tree sap is called _____. (amber, bone)

_____ 5. The fossils found in tar pits are _____. (actual bone, minerals)

_____ 6. An extinct kind of animal is _____. (no longer living, found everywhere)

_____ 7. Fossils show that Earth has _____ over time. (stayed the same, changed)

_____ 8. Fossils show that _____ animals today resemble extinct animals. (some, all)

Applying Strategies: Sequencing

9. Some insects are preserved in amber. The steps are shown here out of order. Using the clue words in the sentences, write the steps in the correct order. (2 points)

Next, the sap completely covers the insect.
Finally, the sap turns into amber.
First, an insect is trapped in sticky sap.

_____

_____

_____

Comparing Animal Traits

A graph helps you compare numbers and amounts. Read the graph. Then answer the questions.

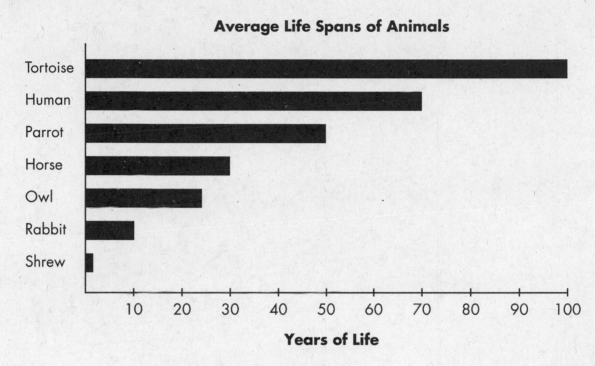

Average Life Spans of Animals

1. How long do most horses live?

_____

2. Which usually lives longer, a human or a parrot?

_____

3. Which animal on the graph lives the longest?

_____

4. A rabbit lives 10 times longer than what animal?

_____

5. How much longer can you expect to live than a horse?

_____

Notes for Home: Your child learned to read a bar graph to compare data about animals.
Home Activity: Make a bar graph comparing the heights of members in your family. Have your child answer questions you ask about the graph.

Notes

Dear Family,

Your child is learning about the lives of different animals. In the science chapter How Animals Live, our class has learned how animals are grouped and about their life cycles. Students have also learned how adaptations help animals live and how fossils tell about animals that lived long ago.

In addition to learning how animals live, grow, and survive, students have also learned many new vocabulary words. Help your child to make these words a part of his or her own vocabulary by using them when you talk together about animals.

trait
vertebrate
larva
pupa
adaptation
inherited
migrate
hibernate

The following pages include activities that you and your child can do together. By participating in your child's education, you will help to bring the learning home.

© Pearson Education, Inc.

Family Science Activity
Play Porcupine

Materials:

- a potato or piece of clay
- markers for coloring
- toothpicks

Steps

1. Use a marker to draw small dots on the surface of the potato or piece of clay. Leave a small area without dots for the head of the porcupine.

2. Take turns pushing toothpicks into the potato or clay. Use the dots you made as a guide. Be careful not to poke yourself. The toothpicks will be the sharp quills of your play porcupine.

3. Use a marker to draw your porcupine's nose, eyes, mouth and ears. You may also look at page 50 of the textbook to see what a porcupine looks like.

4. The porcupine's sharp quills stand up when the porcupine is scared or threatened. The porcupine's quills help protect it. This is called an adaption. Discuss other animals and adaptations they have to protect themselves.

Literacy and Art

Animals need shelter. For example, birds build nests for shelter. Draw a picture of an animal. Be sure to draw shelter for the animal. Then, write 2 or 3 details about the animal and where it lives.

Animal Adaptations

Look at the pictures and words below. **Draw** lines to match each animal with the phrase that describes its adaptation.

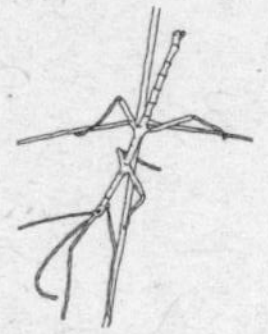

has sharp quills

sprays a bad smell

has sharp claws

has sharp teeth

looks like a twig

can sting

Name _____

Use the words to fill in the map and show how the words are related to each other.

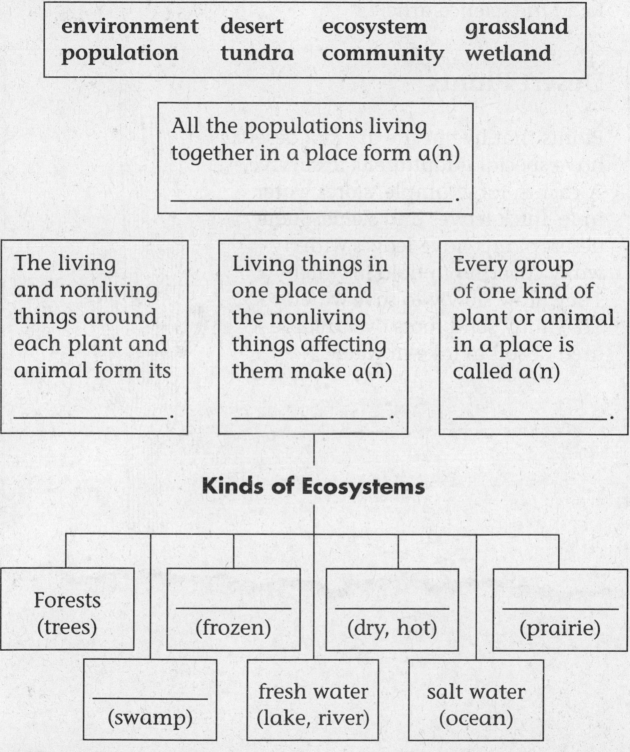

| environment | desert | ecosystem | grassland |
| population | tundra | community | wetland |

All the populations living together in a place form a(n)

_____.

The living and nonliving things around each plant and animal form its

_____.

Living things in one place and the nonliving things affecting them make a(n)

_____.

Every group of one kind of plant or animal in a place is called a(n)

_____.

Kinds of Ecosystems

Forests (trees)

_____ (frozen)

_____ (dry, hot)

_____ (prairie)

_____ (swamp)

fresh water (lake, river)

salt water (ocean)

Notes for Home: Your child learned the vocabulary terms for Chapter 3.
Home Activity: Talk with your child about the kinds of ecosystems. Then identify the type of ecosystem that is found nearest your home, or find magazine pictures showing a type of ecosystem.

Main Idea and Details

Read the science article.

Desert Plants

Plants that live in the dry, hot desert have special adaptations to survive. A cactus, for example, stores water in its thick leaves and stems. Some desert plants have leaves with a waxy covering to hold in water. They grow slowly to save water. They may send roots over a large area of soil to take in water.

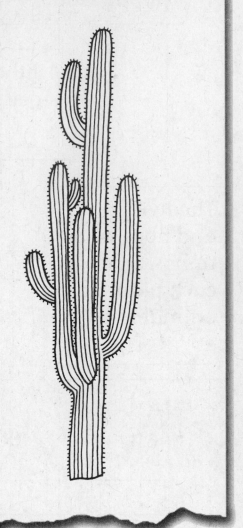

Apply It!

In the outer squares, write details that support the main idea in the center circle.

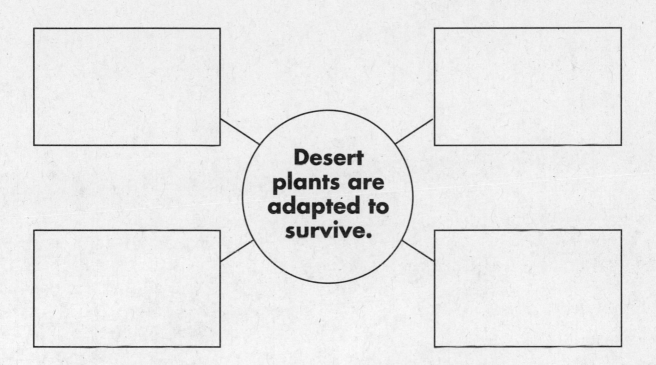

Desert plants are adapted to survive.

© Pearson Education, Inc.

Notes for Home: Your child learned to identify details that support a main idea.
Home Activity: Read an article about plants or animals with your child. State one main idea of the article. Have your child point out details that support that main idea.

Notes

Name _____

Lesson 1: What are ecosystems?

Before You Read Lesson 1

Read each statement below. Place a check mark in the circle to indicate whether you agree or disagree with the statement.

	Agree	Disagree
1. Environment is the nonliving things around you.	○	○
2. Parts of an ecosystem interact.	○	○
3. A population is all the animals in an area.	○	○

After You Read Lesson 1

Reread each statement above. If the lesson supports your choice, place a check mark in the *Correct* circle. Then explain how the text supports your choice. If the lesson does not support your choice, place a check mark in the *Incorrect* circle. Then explain why your choice is wrong.

	Correct	Incorrect
1. _____ _____	○	○
2. _____ _____	○	○
3. _____ _____	○	○

Notes for Home: Your child has completed a pre/post inventory of key concepts in the lesson.
Home Activity: Talk with your child about the ways your community is different from a community in an ecosystem such as a wetland.

© Pearson Education, Inc.

Reviewing Terms: Matching

Match each description with the correct word. Write the letter
on the line next to each description.

_____ 1. everything that surrounds a
living thing

_____ 2. the living and nonliving parts
that interact in an environment

_____ 3. all of the living things of the
same kind that live in the same
place at the same time

_____ 4. all of the populations that live
in the same place

a. population

b. environment

c. community

d. ecosystem

Reviewing Concepts: True or False

Write **T** (True) or **F** (False) on the line before each statement.

_____ 5. Ecosystems are made up of only living parts.

_____ 6. Living parts of ecosystems depend on one another.

_____ 7. A change in a habitat does not affect the living
things in that habitat.

_____ 8. If the plants in an ecosystem die, the animals in the
ecosystem will not have enough food.

Applying Concepts: Main Idea and Details

Use complete sentences to answer question 9. (2 points)

9. List three details you would use to support the main idea
shown here.
Main Idea: Ecosystems change over time.

Detail: _____

Detail: _____

Detail: _____

Lesson 2: Which ecosystems have few trees?

Before You Read Lesson 2

Read each statement below. Place a check mark in the circle to indicate whether you agree or disagree with the statement.

	Agree	Disagree
1. A grassland is a prairie.	○	○
2. A desert is hot by day and cold by night.	○	○
3. A tundra is too cold for big animals.	○	○

After You Read Lesson 2

Reread each statement above. If the lesson supports your choice, place a check mark in the *Correct* circle. Then explain how the text supports your choice. If the lesson does not support your choice, place a check mark in the *Incorrect* circle. Then explain why your choice is wrong.

	Correct	Incorrect
1. _____	○	○
_____		
2. _____	○	○
_____		
3. _____	○	○
_____		

Notes for Home: Your child has completed a pre/post inventory of key concepts in the lesson.
Home Activity: Identify a land ecosystem found in your area. Together list the plants, animals, and objects that you and your child have seen there.

Reviewing Terms: Matching

Match each description with the correct word. Write the letter on the line next to each description.

_____ 1. a land ecosystem with grasses and flowering plants

_____ 2. a land ecosystem that gets very little rain

_____ 3. a cold, dry land ecosystem

a. tundra

b. desert

c. grassland

Reviewing Concepts: Sentence Completion

Complete each sentence with the correct word.

_____ 4. Grasses survive in grasslands because they have _____ roots. (deep, shallow).

_____ 5. Cactuses are plants found in _____. (deserts, grasslands)

_____ 6. Desert plants can live with very little _____. (sunlight, rainfall)

_____ 7. Winters in the _____ are long and cold. (desert, tundra)

_____ 8. In the tundra, soil below the surface stays _____ all year. (wet, frozen)

Applying Strategies: Compare and Contrast

Use complete sentences to answer question 9. (2 points)

9. Name one way in which deserts, tundra, and grasslands are all alike and one way in which they are different.

_____

_____

_____

_____

Lesson 3: What are some forest ecosystems?

Before You Read Lesson 3

Read each statement below. Place a check mark in the circle to indicate whether you agree or disagree with the statement.

	Agree	Disagree
1. Tropical forests lie near the equator.	○	○
2. Trees in deciduous forests drop their leaves in fall.	○	○
3. Coniferous forests get the most rain.	○	○

After You Read Lesson 3

Reread each statement above. If the lesson supports your choice, place a check mark in the *Correct* circle. Then explain how the text supports your choice. If the lesson does not support your choice, place a check mark in the *Incorrect* circle. Then explain why your choice is wrong.

	Correct	Incorrect
1. _____	○	○
_____		
2. _____	○	○
_____		
3. _____	○	○
_____		

Notes for Home: Your child has completed a pre/post inventory of key concepts in the lesson.
Home Activity: With your child, observe some evergreen needles and some broadleaf leaves. Ask your child to tell how they are different.

Reviewing Concepts: Matching

Match each description with the correct kind of forest. Write the letter on the line next to each description. You can use each answer more than once.

_____ 1. These grow mainly in northern North America, Europe, and Asia.

_____ 2. Oak, maple, and beech trees are found in these.

_____ 3. These have a climate that is warm and rainy all year long.

_____ 4. Spruce, fir, and pine trees are found in these.

_____ 5. Trees with leaves that look like needles are found in these.

_____ 6. Mosses and lichens are some of the things that can live on the floor of these.

_____ 7. These grow near the equator.

_____ 8. Sunlight reaches the forest floor during a part of the year in these.

a. coniferous forests

b. deciduous forests

c. tropical forests

Applying Strategies: Converting Units

9. A tropical rainforest gets an average of 300 centimeters of rain each year. How many meters of rain is this? There are 100 centimeters in 1 meter. Show your work. (2 points)

_____

_____

_____

Lesson 4: What are water ecosystems?

Before You Read Lesson 4

Read each statement below. Place a check mark in the circle to indicate whether you agree or disagree with the statement.

	Agree	Disagree
1. A wetland is a freshwater ecosystem.	○	○
2. Most life in the oceans is at the bottom.	○	○
3. Saltwater ecosystems cover most of the world.	○	○

After You Read Lesson 4

Reread each statement above. If the lesson supports your choice, place a check mark in the *Correct* circle. Then explain how the text supports your choice. If the lesson does not support your choice, place a check mark in the *Incorrect* circle. Then explain why your choice is wrong.

	Correct	Incorrect
1. _____ _____	○	○
2. _____ _____	○	○
3. _____ _____	○	○

Notes for Home: Your child has completed a pre/post inventory of key concepts in the lesson.
Home Activity: With your child, observe an aquarium (or read about setting one up). Together list the things needed for this freshwater ecosystem.

Reviewing Terms: Sentence Completion

Complete each sentence with the correct word or phrase.

_____ 1. A low land covered by water at least part of the year is a _____. (wetland, tropical forest)

Reviewing Concepts: True or False

Write **T** (True) or **F** (False) on the line before each statement.

_____ 2. Lakes, ponds, and rivers are usually saltwater ecosystems.

_____ 3. Rivers and streams are moving water.

_____ 4. Water flows very quickly through the Everglades in Florida.

_____ 5. Animals do not live in the Everglades.

_____ 6. Ocean water is salt water.

_____ 7. Most living things in the ocean live at the very bottom.

_____ 8. Salt marshes form where river water mixes with ocean water.

Writing

Use complete sentences to answer question 9. (2 points)

9. Describe two ways that wetlands are important to animals.

_____

_____

_____

_____

Comparing Data

Look at the graph. Use it to answer the questions.

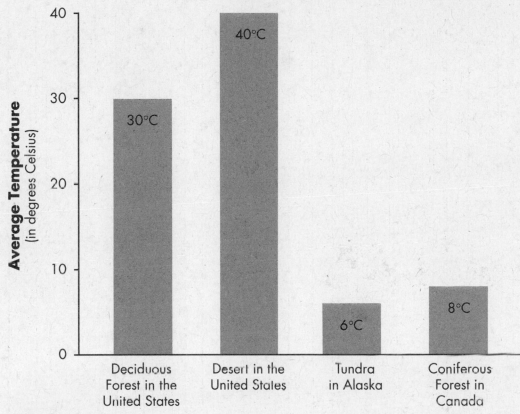

Average Summer Temperatures in Different Ecosystems

Questions

1. Which ecosystem is hottest?

   _____

2. Which ecosystem is coldest?

   _____

3. Which ecosystems have very close temperatures?

   _____

Notes for Home: Your child learned how to read and use a graph.
Home Activity: Find a graph in a newspaper or magazine. Review the data with
your child and ask questions about the data.

Notes

Dear Family,

Your child is learning about different environments where plants and animals live together. In the science chapter Where Plants and Animals Live, our class has learned about land ecosystems, including some with few trees and others with forests. The children have also learned about water ecosystems, such as rivers, salt marshes, and oceans.

In addition to learning where plants and animals live, the children have also learned many new vocabulary words. Help your child to make these words a part of his or her own vocabulary by using them when you talk together about different ecosystems.

environment
ecosystem
population
community
grassland
desert
tundra
wetland

The following pages include activities that you and your child can do together. By participating in your child's education, you will help to bring the learning home.

© Pearson Education, Inc.

Family Science Activity
At Home in a Forest Ecosystem

Materials:

- colored pencils and markers
- white drawing paper

Steps:

1. Talk with your child about forests. Have you been to a forest? What kinds of plants and animals did you see? Have you seen any of these plants and animals?

2. Read the following list of plants and animals.
   Plants: oak trees, evergreen trees, shrubs
   Animals: woodpeckers, rabbits, foxes, beavers, deer, bears

3. Dicuss the forest ecosystem. The forest has large plants such as oak trees that create shade for small plants. The plants provide habitat for small animals. Large animals such as foxes and bears survive by eating plants and smaller animals.

4. Have your child draw a scene of a forest on a sheet of drawing paper. They may copy or trace pictures from page 2 of this booklet. Your child can also draw nonliving things that are part of the forest ecosystem, such as rocks, soil and water.

5. Ask your child to label each plant and animal in the drawing. Encourage your child to explain the drawing and display the picture for others to see.

Workbook

Look at the pictures and words below.
Draw lines to match the pictures and words.

oak tree

evergreen tree

shrub

rabbit

fox

bear

What Is There?

Write the name of one living thing and one nonliving thing that you can find in each one of these ecosystems.

Grassland

Desert

Tundra

Forest

Wetland

Ocean

Name _____

Think about each word or set of words. Write the words to complete the outline.

I. germs

   A. What do they do? Germs cause _____.

   B. Examples of germs: _____

II. producer, consumer, predator, prey

   A. How do they get food? _____ make their

      own food. _____ eat food.

   B. Who eats whom? A _____ eats other

      animals, which are called _____.

III. herbivore, carnivore, omnivore

   A. How are they alike? They are all types of _____.

   B. How are they different? _____ eat only

      plants. _____ eat only animals.

      _____ eat both plants and animals.

IV. competition

   A. What is it? _____

      _____

   B. When does it happen? _____

      _____

Notes for Home: Your child learned the vocabulary terms for Chapter 4.
Home Activity: Have your child cut out magazine pictures or draw pictures to illustrate each vocabulary term.

© Pearson Education, Inc.

Draw Conclusions

Read the paragraph.

Jose Becomes Ill

Jose is beginning to get a fever and a sore throat. Last week, his little sister had a cold. They usually play with the same toys at home.

Apply It!

Write facts from the paragraph in the small boxes on the next page. Then write your conclusion in the big box.

Name _____

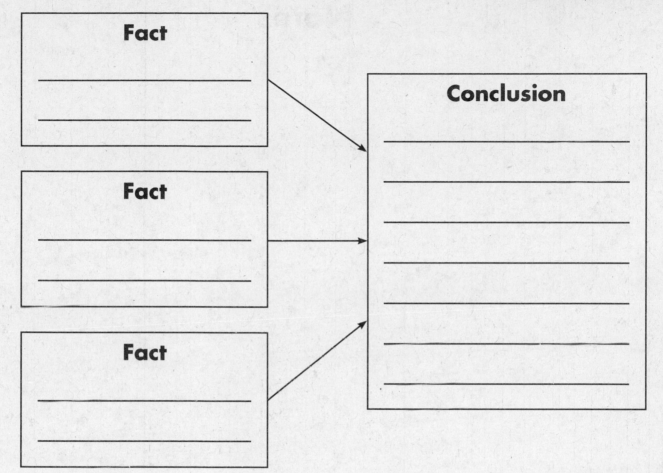

Fact

_____

_____

Fact

_____

_____

Fact

_____

_____

Conclusion

_____

_____

_____

_____

_____

_____

_____

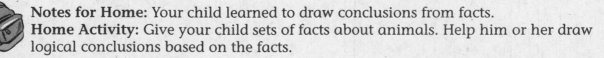

Notes for Home: Your child learned to draw conclusions from facts.
Home Activity: Give your child sets of facts about animals. Help him or her draw logical conclusions based on the facts.

© Pearson Education, Inc.

Notes

Name _____

Lesson 1: How do living things interact?

Before You Read Lesson 1

Read each statement below. Place a check mark in the circle to indicate whether you agree or disagree with the statement.

	Agree	Disagree
1. Animals may live in groups to protect each other.	○	○
2. A bee visits a flower, and both benefit.	○	○
3. Different kinds of living things do not help each other.	○	○

After You Read Lesson 1

Reread each statement above. If the lesson supports your choice, place a check mark in the *Correct* circle. Then explain how the text supports your choice. If the lesson does not support your choice, place a check mark in the *Incorrect* circle. Then explain why your choice is wrong.

	Correct	Incorrect
1. _____	○	○
_____		
2. _____	○	○
_____		
3. _____	○	○

Notes for Home: Your child has completed a pre/post inventory of key concepts in the lesson.
Home Activity: Together observe an animal interaction, such as a pet getting food from you. Talk about how the interaction helps the animal(s) survive.

Reviewing Concepts: Matching

Match the examples with the correct description of the way living things interact. Write the letter on the line next to each description. You can use each answer more than once.

_____ 1. members of a herd protecting each other

_____ 2. a cleaner fish getting food when it cleans a larger fish

_____ 3. a bee "dancing" to show other bees where flowers are

_____ 4. a tree helping a flower get light, the flower does not help or harm the tree

_____ 5. a prairie dog whistling to warn its group of predators

_____ 6. a bee getting food when it pollinates a flower

_____ 7. barnacles living on whales, the whales are not helped or harmed

_____ 8. a moth pollinating a yucca plant and laying its eggs in the plant

a. helping in groups

b. one kind helping another

c. two kinds helping each other

Applying Concepts: Draw Conclusions

Use complete sentences to answer question 9. (2 points)

9. Read the three facts below. Then write a conclusion that is supported by the facts.

Fact 1: Sometimes animals help others in their group.

Fact 2: Sometimes one kind of animal helps another kind.

Fact 3: Sometimes two kinds of animals help each other.

Conclusion: _____

_____

Lesson 2: How do living things get energy?

Before You Read Lesson 2

Read each statement below. Place a check mark in the circle to indicate whether you agree or disagree with the statement.

	Agree	Disagree
1. All animals are consumers.	○	○
2. Producers get their energy from food.	○	○
3. Many food chains make a food web.	○	○

After You Read Lesson 2

Reread each statement above. If the lesson supports your choice, place a check mark in the *Correct* circle. Then explain how the text supports your choice. If the lesson does not support your choice, place a check mark in the *Incorrect* circle. Then explain why your choice is wrong.

	Correct	Incorrect
1. _____	○	○
_____		
2. _____	○	○
_____		
3. _____	○	○
_____		

Notes for Home: Your child has completed a pre/post inventory of key concepts in the lesson.
Home Activity: List some foods your family has eaten today. Have your child classify them as plant or animal. Talk about where each got its energy from.

Reviewing Terms: Matching

Match each description with the correct word. Write the letter on the line next to each description.

_____ 1. a living thing that makes food   **a.** prey

_____ 2. a living thing that eats food   **b.** consumer

_____ 3. a consumer that eats only plants   **c.** omnivore

_____ 4. a consumer that eats only animals   **d.** predator

                                 e. producer

_____ 5. a consumer that eats both plants and animals   **f.** herbivore

                                 g. carnivore

_____ 6. any animal that is hunted by others for food

_____ 7. a consumer that hunts for food

Reviewing Concepts: Sentence Completion

Complete the sentence with the correct word.

_____ 8. Food chains and food webs show how _____ moves between living things. (water, energy)

Applying Strategies: Calculating

9. In one food chain, ferrets eat prairie dogs. If each ferret eats 4 prairie dogs each month, how many prairie dogs would be eaten by 11 ferrets in one month? Show your work. (2 points)

Lesson 3: How do living things compete?

Before You Read Lesson 3

Read each statement below. Place a check mark in the circle to indicate whether you agree or disagree with the statement.

	Agree	Disagree
1. Animals compete, but plants do not.	○	○
2. Two predators might compete for prey.	○	○
3. Living things compete for food, water, and space.	○	○

After You Read Lesson 3

Reread each statement above. If the lesson supports your choice, place a check mark in the *Correct* circle. Then explain how the text supports your choice. If the lesson does not support your choice, place a check mark in the *Incorrect* circle. Then explain why your choice is wrong.

	Correct	Incorrect
1. _____ _____	○	○
2. _____ _____	○	○
3. _____ _____	○	○

Notes for Home: Your child has completed a pre/post inventory of key concepts in the lesson.
Home Activity: Observe some plants near your home. Discuss with your child how they are competing for the same space, food, and water and predict which will win.

Reviewing Terms: Sentence Completion

Complete each sentence with the correct word.

_____ 1. When two or more living things need the same resources, they are in _____ with one another. (cooperation, competition)

Reviewing Concepts: True or False

Write **T** (True) or **F** (False) on the line before each statement.

_____ 2. Living things compete for many kinds of resources.

_____ 3. Animals do not compete for mates.

_____ 4. Animals that are good predators pass those traits to their young.

_____ 5. Prey often compete to get predators.

_____ 6. Sometimes people and animals compete for space.

_____ 7. Some living things compete for oxygen.

_____ 8. Competition between animals sometimes follows cycles.

Writing

Use complete sentences to answer question 9. (2 points)

9. Write a short paragraph that describes two kinds of birds competing for a resource they both need to survive.

_____

_____

_____

_____

_____

Lesson 4: How do environments change?

Before You Read Lesson 4

Read each statement below. Place a check mark in the circle to indicate whether you agree or disagree with the statement.

	Agree	Disagree
1. Living things can change their environment.	○	○
2. Fire destroys a forest forever.	○	○
3. Environment changes often occur in patterns.	○	○

After You Read Lesson 4

Reread each statement above. If the lesson supports your choice, place a check mark in the *Correct* circle. Then explain how the text supports your choice. If the lesson does not support your choice, place a check mark in the *Incorrect* circle. Then explain why your choice is wrong.

	Correct	Incorrect
1. _____	○	○
2. _____	○	○
3. _____	○	○

Notes for Home: Your child has completed a pre/post inventory of key concepts in the lesson.
Home Activity: Point out a community environment that has changed, such as a construction site. Ask your child how this change affected the organisms that live there.

© Pearson Education, Inc.

Name _____

Reviewing Terms: Sentence Completion

Complete each sentence with the correct word.

_____ 1. A living thing that breaks down waste and living things that have died is a _____. (decomposer, decay)

_____ 2. _____ is the process of breaking down waste and living things that have died. (Decomposer, Decay)

Reviewing Concepts: Matching

Living things and natural events can cause environments to change. For each description of change listed below, show whether it is a change caused by a living thing or a natural event. You can use each answer more than once.

_____ 3. A volcano erupts and kills plants in an environment.

_____ 4. A hurricane knocks down trees.

_____ 5. A forest fire burns plants and trees.

_____ 6. A person chops down trees to make space to build a house.

_____ 7. A drought causes many plants to die.

_____ 8. A beaver's dam floods an area.

a. a living thing

b. a natural event

Applying Strategies: Cause and Effect

Use complete sentences to answer question 9. (2 points)

9. Write three causes of environmental change.

Cause: _____

Cause: _____

Cause: _____

Effect: An environment is changed.

Workbook

Lesson 5: What is a healthy environment for people?

Before You Read Lesson 5

Read each statement below. Place a check mark in the circle to indicate whether you agree or disagree with the statement.

	Agree	Disagree
1. Food and water are all people need to live.	○	○
2. To get needed nutrients, we should eat a variety of foods.	○	○
3. Dairy products help grow strong bones.	○	○

After You Read Lesson 5

Reread each statement above. If the lesson supports your choice, place a check mark in the *Correct* circle. Then explain how the text supports your choice. If the lesson does not support your choice, place a check mark in the *Incorrect* circle. Then explain why your choice is wrong.

	Correct	Incorrect
1. _____ _____	○	○
2. _____ _____	○	○
3. _____	○	○

Notes for Home: Your child has completed a pre/post inventory of key concepts in the lesson.
Home Activity: Plan a healthful lunch with your child. Together prepare the meal. Enjoy your lunch as you discuss the importance of eating a variety of foods.

Reviewing Concepts: True or False

Write **T** (True) or **F** (False) on the line before each statement.

_____ 1. People need food to survive.

_____ 2. Not all people need water.

_____ 3. People need to live in a clean environment.

_____ 4. Shelter helps people stay at a comfortable temperature.

_____ 5. Only people in cities need air to live.

_____ 6. Eating a variety of foods helps people stay healthy.

_____ 7. People who handle food should have clean hands.

_____ 8. The digestive system takes in the air people need to live.

Applying Strategies: Sequencing

Use complete sentences to answer question 9. (2 points)

9. The steps of what happens to food in the digestive system are shown out of order. Using the clue words in the sentences, write the steps in the correct order.

   Next, food is mixed with digestive juices in the stomach.
   Finally, solid waste is formed in the large intestine.
   First, the teeth break food into pieces.
   Then food particles pass into the bloodstream through the small intestine walls.

_____

_____

_____

_____

© Pearson Education, Inc.

Name _____

Think, Read, Learn

Use with pages 124–127.

Lesson 6: How can people stay healthy?

Before You Read Lesson 6

Read each statement below. Place a check mark in the circle to indicate whether you agree or disagree with the statement.

	Agree	Disagree
1. Exercise helps the heart, lungs, and muscles.	○	○
2. Your lungs are part of your circulatory system.	○	○
3. Bacteria and viruses are germs.	○	○

After You Read Lesson 6

Reread each statement above. If the lesson supports your choice, place a check mark in the *Correct* circle. Then explain how the text supports your choice. If the lesson does not support your choice, place a check mark in the *Incorrect* circle. Then explain why your choice is wrong.

	Correct	Incorrect
1. _____ _____	○	○
2. _____ _____	○	○
3. _____ _____	○	○

Notes for Home: Your child has completed a pre/post inventory of key concepts in the lesson.
Home Activity: Talk with your child about a time he or she became ill. Discuss how it happened and what you did to help your child get better.

© Pearson Education, Inc.

Reviewing Terms: Matching

Match each description with the correct word or phrase. Write the letter on the line next to each description.

_____ 1. very small living things or particles that can cause disease

a. diseases

b. germs

_____ 2. conditions in which parts of the body do not work properly

Reviewing Concepts: Sentence Completion

Complete each sentence with the correct word.

_____ 3. Sports and yard work are good ways to get _____. (exercise, rest)

_____ 4. Lungs are a part of the _____ system. (respiratory, circulatory)

_____ 5. The heart is a part of the _____ system. (digestive, circulatory)

_____ 6. The windpipe is a tube that leads to the _____. (heart, lungs)

_____ 7. Flu and chicken pox are caused by _____. (germs, exercise)

_____ 8. Exercise and rest can help people stay _____. (sick, healthy)

Applying Strategies: Converting

9. For one week, Tara's family recorded the number of hours and minutes they exercised. By the end of the week, Tara had exercised for 2 hours and 25 minutes. Show the amount of time that Tara exercised in minutes. Remember, 60 minutes are equal to 1 hour. Show your work. (2 points)

Health by the Numbers

Read the cereal labels. Then answer the questions.

Tasty Squares
Serving Size: 1 cup
Calories: 170
Total Fat: 2.0 grams
Cholesterol: 0 grams
Sodium: 180 milligrams
Carbohydrates: 39 grams
Fiber: 3 grams
Sugar: 15 grams

Oaty Bits
Serving Size: 1 cup
Calories: 150
Total Fat: 1.0 grams
Cholesterol: 0 grams
Sodium: 95 milligrams
Carbohydrates: 25 grams
Fiber: 10 grams
Sugar: 11 grams

1. Jeb had two servings of Tasty Squares. How many calories

    did he eat? _____

2. Pauline had three servings of Oaty Bits. How much sodium

    did she eat? _____

3. How many more grams of carbohydrates are in a serving
    of Tasty Squares than in a serving of Oaty Bits?

    _____

4. You should get 25 grams of fiber a day. How many servings
    of each cereal would it take to get 25 grams of fiber?

    Tasty Squares _____

    Oaty Bits _____

Notes for Home: Your child learned to read labels, compare their data, and solve
problems based on the data.
Home Activity: Together compare the labels of several cereals your child eats.
Rank them according to the amount of sugar, and then the amount of fiber.

© Pearson Education, Inc.

Notes

Dear Family,

Your child is learning about different ways that plants and animals interact. In the science chapter Plants and Animals Living Together, our class learned how food energy moves from one living thing to another. We read how plants, animals, and natural events can change environments. Students also learned what people need in order to be healthy and to stay healthy.

In addition to learning how plants and animals interact with their environment, students also learned many new vocabulary words. Help your child to make these words a part of his or her own vocabulary by using them when you talk together about plants and animals living together.

producer	consumer	herbivore
carnivore	omnivore	predator
prey	competition	decomposer
decay	disease	germs

The following pages include activities that you and your child can do together. By participating in your child's education, you will help to bring the learning home.

Family Science Activity
Observing Decomposers at Work

Materials:

- water
- piece of leftover bread or cheese
- piece of leftover fruit or vegetable
- clear glass jar with a lid
- tape

Steps

1. Wet each piece of food and put it into the jar. Make sure that the pieces are not touching. Seal the edge of the lid with tape.

2. Ask your child to predict which decomposers will help break down the food.

3. Draw a chart with two columns. Label each column with one of the foods you put in the jar. Draw seven rows and label them Day 1 through Day 7.

4. Observe the food once a day for a week. As mold grows on the food, ask your child to write down what the mold looks like, where it grows, and what it does.

5. At the end of the week, discuss what you observed with your child. What decomposers did you see? Where did they grow? Did the same kinds of mold grow on both pieces of food? Did they look the same or different?

Vocabulary Practice

Find 9 vocabulary words in the puzzle below
and circle them.

```
R  C  A  R  N  I  V  O  R  E  C
P  R  E  D  A  T  O  R  X  P  O
C  O  M  P  E  T  I  T  I  O  N
U  M  R  Q  O  M  A  J  V  S
D  N  E  E  B  R  G  C  G  U  U
O  I  K  Y  A  C  E  D  L  U  M
R  V  S  I  Z  R  R  K  O  M  E
P  O  Q  B  A  A  M  C  J  F  R
W  R  E  L  D  I  S  E  A  S  E
H  E  R  B  I  V  O  R  E  P  R
```

Kinds of Consumers

What kind of consumer is it? Write if each
animal is an herbivore, a carnivore, or an
omnivore.

Cow:
eats plants

_____

Shark:
eats meat

_____

Rabbit:
eats plants

_____

Person:
eats meat and plants

_____

Wolf:
eats meat

_____

Workbook

Dear Family,

Your child is learning about the ways in which water is important to life on Earth. In the science chapter Water, our class has learned how water changes phases and how it moves around Earth. The children have also learned different ways that people clean water.

In addition to learning about the uses of water, the children have also learned many new vocabulary words. Help your child to make these words a part of his or her own vocabulary by using them when you talk together about water.

water vapor
groundwater
wetlands
evaporation
condensation
water cycle
precipitation

The following pages include activities that you and your child can do together. By participating in your child's education, you will help to bring the learning home.

Family Science Activity
Evaporation Experiments

Materials:

- four identical, disposable plastic cups
- a grease pencil or permanent marker
- plastic wrap
- a rubber band

Steps

1. Talk about evaporation with your child. Evaporation is when water in liquid form goes into the air and becomes a gas called water vapor. Ask your child to predict how heat will affect the evaporation of water.

2. Help your child pour the same amount of water into each plastic cup.

3. Draw a line on each cup with the grease pencil or marker to mark the water level.

4. Cover two of the cups with plastic wrap and put a rubber band around each cup to seal the plastic cover.

5. Put one uncovered cup and one covered cup in a warm place. Put the other two cups in a cool place. Choose places where the water will not be disturbed.

6. Check each cup every day for a week with your child. When the water level in a cup changes, mark the new water level on the cup with the grease pencil or marker.

7. At the end of the week, compare the water levels in the four cups. Talk with your child about how much water evaporated from each cup. How did heat affect the evaporation of water in the uncovered cups? What happened to the water in the covered cups?

Literacy and Art

Look at the picture and words below.
Draw lines to match the pictures and the words.

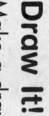

Rain

Water Faucet

River

Snowflake (snow)

Ice

Draw It!

Make a drawing that shows different places we can find water and the different forms it can take.

Name _____

Use the vocabulary words in the box to complete the labels on the diagram. Use your own words to add more examples.

| weather | hurricane | tornado | blizzard |

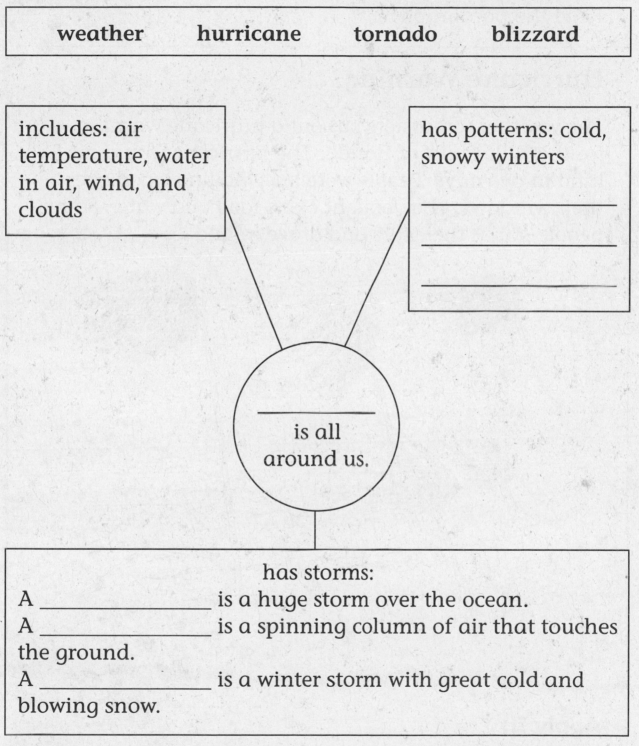

includes: air temperature, water in air, wind, and clouds

has patterns: cold, snowy winters

_____

_____

_____

_____ is all around us.

has storms:

A _____ is a huge storm over the ocean.

A _____ is a spinning column of air that touches the ground.

A _____ is a winter storm with great cold and blowing snow.

Notes for Home: Your child learned the vocabulary terms for Chapter 6.
Home Activity: Talk with your child about today's weather. Take turns making statements about the temperature, wind, clouds, and amount of moisture in the air.

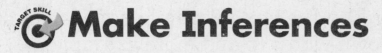
Make Inferences

Read the paragraph.

Hurricane Warning

The weather forecasters put out a hurricane warning for the Gulf Coast of Florida. The hurricane would hit land in two days. People were busy nailing wood over their windows. They bought extra food and water. Some people got in their cars and drove inland.

Apply It!

What inference can you make from the facts in the paragraph? Write the facts and your inference in the graphic organizer on page 55.

Name _____

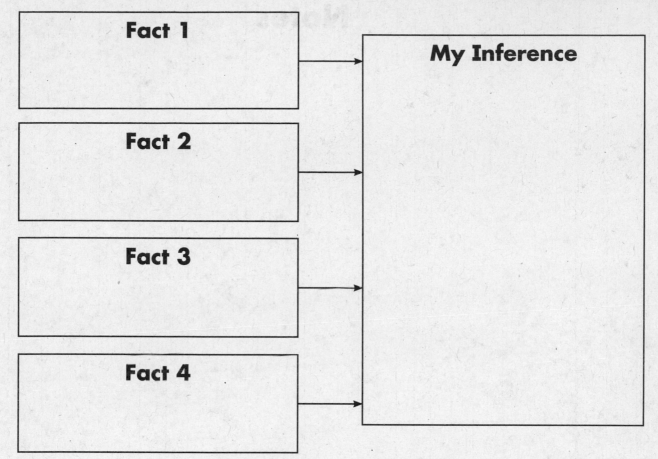

 **Notes for Home:** Your child learned how to evaluate the facts to make an inference.
Home Activity: Describe a situation, for example: "You wake to find the grass wet and puddles on the street." Have your child make an inference about what happened.

Notes

Name _____

Lesson 1: What makes up weather?

Before You Read Lesson 1

Read each statement below. Place a check mark in the circle to indicate whether you agree or disagree with the statement.

	Agree	Disagree
1. Atmosphere is the blanket of gases around the Earth.	○	○
2. A barometer measures wind speed.	○	○
3. Air pressure is low when the air presses down a lot.	○	○

After You Read Lesson 1

Reread each statement above. If the lesson supports your choice, place a check mark in the *Correct* circle. Then explain how the text supports your choice. If the lesson does not support your choice, place a check mark in the *Incorrect* circle. Then explain why your choice is wrong.

	Correct	Incorrect
1. _____	○	○
_____		
2. _____	○	○
_____		
3. _____	○	○
_____		

Notes for Home: Your child has completed a pre-/post-inventory of key concepts in the lesson.
Home Activity: Together watch or read a weather forecast. Talk with your child about a weather pattern that has occurred this week, such as a thunderstorm followed by clear, dry air.

Reviewing Terms: Sentence Completion

Complete each sentence with the correct word.

_____ 1. The blanket of air that surrounds Earth is the _____. (anemometer, atmosphere)

_____ 2. _____ is the temperature, clouds, precipitation, and wind conditions in an area. (Weather, Pollution)

Reviewing Concepts: True or False

Write **T** (True) or **F** (False) on the line before each statement.

_____ 3. Clouds are made up of water droplets in the air.

_____ 4. There is one kind of cloud.

_____ 5. Earth's atmosphere has layers that have different temperatures than one another.

_____ 6. The force of the atmosphere pressing down is called air pressure.

_____ 7. Humidity is the amount of water vapor in the air.

_____ 8. Weather data can be gathered with satellites.

Applying Strategies: Making Inferences

Use complete sentences to answer question 9. (2 points)

9. Terry checked the barometer reading several times during the day. The barometer reading was lower each time she checked. What does a barometer measure? What weather conditions could Terry expect?

_____

_____

_____

Name _____

Lesson 2: How does weather affect people?

Before You Read Lesson 2

Read each statement below. Place a check mark in the circle to indicate whether you agree or disagree with the statement.

	Agree	Disagree
1. In most places, the weather changes in a pattern.	○	○
2. A blizzard is a dangerous winter storm.	○	○
3. A hurricane is a spinning cloud on the ground.	○	○

After You Read Lesson 2

Reread each statement above. If the lesson supports your choice, place a check mark in the *Correct* circle. Then explain how the text supports your choice. If the lesson does not support your choice, place a check mark in the *Incorrect* circle. Then explain why your choice is wrong.

	Correct	Incorrect
1. _____	○	○
_____		
2. _____	○	○
_____		
3. _____	○	○
_____		

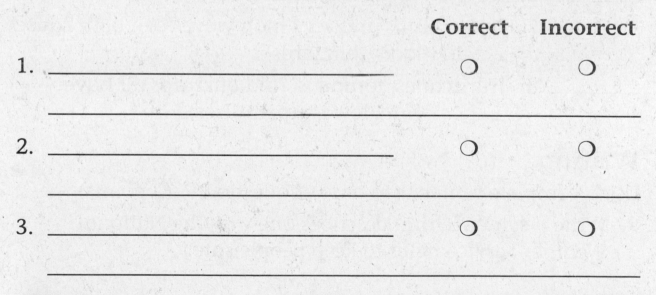

Notes for Home: Your child has completed a pre-/post-inventory of key concepts in the lesson.
Home Activity: Talk with your child about a storm that can occur in your area (thunderstorm, hurricane, tornado, blizzard). List safety tips and ways to prepare for the storm.

© Pearson Education, Inc.

Name _____

Reviewing Terms: Matching

Match each definition with the correct word. Write the letter on the line next to each definition.

_____ 1. a winter storm with blowing snow

_____ 2. a storm with a funnel-shaped column of air that touches the ground

_____ 3. storms with heavy rain, strong winds, and huge waves

a. hurricane
b. blizzard
c. tornado

Reviewing Concepts: Sentence Completion

Complete the sentence with the correct word or phrase.

_____ 4. Patterns of weather are _____ everywhere on Earth. (different, the same)

_____ 5. As air moves up a mountain it gets _____. (colder, wetter)

_____ 6. All deserts are _____. (hot, dry)

_____ 7. Heavy rains and very high waves can both cause _____. (floods, blizzards)

_____ 8. Hurricanes, tornados, and blizzards all have _____. (wind, low temperatures)

Writing

Use a complete sentence to answer question 9. (2 points)

9. Write a sentence that describes one way the National Weather Service helps to keep people safe.

_____

_____

_____

Comparing Temperatures

The table shows temperatures for the town of Smithport. Each temperature represents the average daytime high for July in a certain year. Do you see a pattern?

Changes in High Temperature for Smithport, 1980–2005

Year	1980	1985	1990	1995	2000	2005
Average daytime high for July	79°	79°	81°	80°	83°	84°

Use the table to answer these questions.

1. What trend, or pattern, do you see happening over 25 years?

   _____

2. When did the biggest change occur?

   _____

3. How much warmer was it, on average, in July in Smithport in 2000 than in 1985?

   _____

4. What could explain the change?

   _____

   _____

   _____

   _____

Notes for Home: Your child learned how to read a table to compare data.
Home Activity: Help your child make a table showing the high temperature every day for a week. Talk about any pattern you see.

Notes

Dear Family,

Your child is learning about the weather and how it can affect our lives. In the science chapter Weather, our class has learned about weather patterns, instruments scientists use to measure the weather, and different types of storms. They have also been studying the atmosphere, the blanket of air that surrounds Earth. Finally, we have looked at weather maps and discussed high and low temperatures.

In addition to learning about weather, the students have also learned many new vocabulary words. Help your child to make these words a part of his or her own vocabulary by using them when you talk together about the weather.

weather
atmosphere
hurricane
tornado
blizzard

The following pages include activities that you and your child can do together. By participating in your child's education, you will help to bring the learning home.

Family Science Activity
Draw a Weather Report

Materials:

- newspaper, radio, or television
- white paper
- ruler
- colored pencils or markers

Steps

1. Watch or listen to a weather forecast together at home.

2. Discuss the weather conditions for today and the next few days. Will it be sunny, cloudy or rainy? Is a storm coming? Ask your child to read or listen for the barometric pressure. Discuss that if the barometric pressure is low, the weather may be cloudy or rainy. If the pressure is high, the skies may be clear.

3. Have your child pretend that he or she is a weather forecaster. Invite your child to draw three boxes on a piece of white paper, using a ruler.

4. Ask your child to draw a picture of the weather forecast for the following three days. This can be an imaginary forecast or based on the actual forecast.

5. Encourage your child to write in the **High Temperature** and **Low Temperature** for each day and whether the barometric pressure is high or low or changing.

6. Ask your child to explain the weather drawing to you and give a weather report. Display the weather forecast in your home.

Workbook

Weather Words

Look for the words in the puzzle and circle them.

atmosphere	blizzard	hurricane
tornado	weather	

```
H U R R I C A N E W
V Y U E H G Y V B E
B D T O R N A D O A
L B P R K M X G I T
I O R D A S T M U H
Z O R J C P R L Y E
N N V L K V J Q R
A T M O S P H E R E
R G V T O A S E W R
D I S E H M A E W E
```

Extreme Weather

Hurricanes, tornadoes, and blizzards can bring strong rain, winds, or snow. Read the words in the box and write them where they belong in the table.

snow	storm	funnel
oceans	Strong	waves

Hurricanes	Tornadoes	Blizzards
Huge storms that form over _____	Spinning _____ shaped columns of air	A winter _____
Heavy rain, strong winds, and huge _____	_____ winds	Blowing _____ in the ocean

Workbook

Name _____

Read the clues. Choose a word to answer each riddle.

rock	metamorphic rock	igneous rock
mineral	sedimentary rock	decay
soil	nutrient	loam

1. Granite is an example. It forms deep underground. It needs heat to form. What is it? _____

2. When they die, plants and animals do this. It means to break down into bits. What is it? _____

3. It covers most of the land on Earth. It is made up of bits of rock and dead plant and animal matter. It is a home to earthworms. What is it? _____

4. It is a natural material. It has never been living. Every rock contains at least one. What is it? _____

5. Heat and pressure made it what it is today. Its name means "changes form." Slate is an example. What is it?

   _____

6. It is a kind of soil. Plants grow well in it. It holds lots of water. It is a mixture. What is it? _____

7. It forms in layers. It might contain fossils. It can tell a "story" about how life has changed over time. What is it?

   _____

8. A mountain is mostly this. It is solid and nonliving. It contains one or more minerals. It can be placed in one of three main groups. What is it? _____

9. It is a material that plants take from soil. It helps plants grow. It might come from a mineral or decaying plants and animals. What is it? _____

Notes for Home: Your child learned the vocabulary terms for Chapter 7.
Home Activity: Have your child cut out magazine pictures or draw pictures that illustrate the vocabulary words. Make up sentences together that use the words.

© Pearson Education, Inc.

Compare and Contrast

Read the magazine article and look at the pictures. How are rocks and soil alike and different?

Rocks and Soil

The solid surface of Earth is covered with rocks and soil. Rocks are made of one or more minerals. Minerals are natural nonliving materials. Rocks may be large or small, but they are solid and hard to break. When rocks break down, soil can start to form. Soil is a loose mix of tiny bits of rock and material from dead plants and animals. Water will soak up into soil, but it runs off of rock.

Apply It!

Use the graphic organizer on the next page to compare rocks with soil.

Name _____

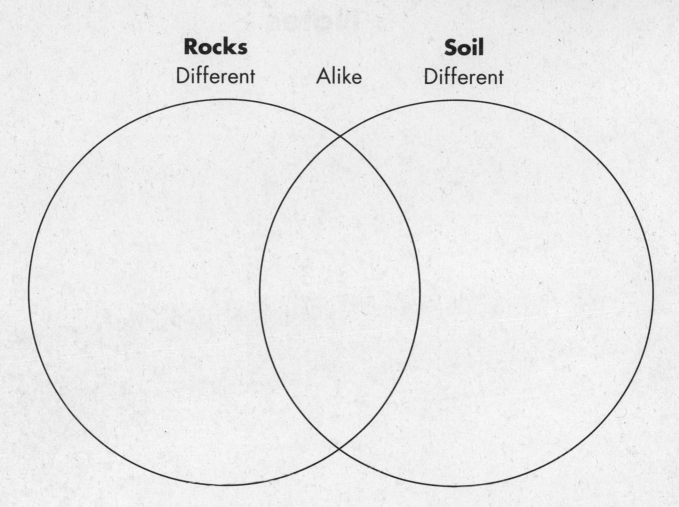

Rocks
Different   Alike   **Soil**
                                  Different

© Pearson Education, Inc.

Notes for Home: Your child learned about the skill of comparing and contrasting.
Home Activity: With your child make your own Venn diagram comparing and
contrasting two familiar things, such as two pets or two favorite foods.

Notes

Lesson 1: How do rocks form?

Before You Read Lesson 1

Read each statement below. Place a check mark in the circle to indicate whether you agree or disagree with the statement.

	Agree	Disagree
1. Rocks are made of one or more minerals.	○	○
2. Igneous rock forms in layers.	○	○
3. Fossils are usually found in metamorphic rock.	○	○

After You Read Lesson 1

Reread each statement above. If the lesson supports your choice, place a check mark in the *Correct* circle. Then explain how the text supports your choice. If the lesson does not support your choice, place a check mark in the *Incorrect* circle. Then explain why your choice is wrong.

	Correct	Incorrect
1. _____	○	○
_____		
2. _____	○	○
_____		
3. _____	○	○
_____		

Notes for Home: Your child has completed a pre/post inventory of key concepts in the lesson.
Home Activity: Gather stones and sort them into groups according to similarities. Use the words *color, texture,* and *minerals* to describe the rock groups.

Name _____

Reviewing Terms: Matching

Match each description with the correct word or phrase. Write the letter on the line next to each description.

_____ 1. any solid, nonliving material made of one or more mineral

_____ 2. a natural material that forms from nonliving matter

_____ 3. a rock that forms from a mixture of melted material and gases

_____ 4. a rock made of layers that are cemented together

_____ 5. a rock that has been changed by heat and pressure

a. sedimentary rock

b. igneous rock

c. rock

d. mineral

e. metamorphic rock

Reviewing Concepts: True or False

Write **T** (True) or **F** (False) on the line before each statement.

_____ 6. All rocks have the same texture and grain size.

_____ 7. Fossils are most often found in metamorphic rock.

_____ 8. Igneous rock can come from volcanoes.

Applying Concepts: Compare and Contrast

Use complete sentences to answer question 9. (2 points)

9. Name one way in which sedimentary, igneous, and metamorphic rocks are similar and one way in which they are different.

_____

_____

_____

© Pearson Education, Inc.

Lesson 2: What are minerals?

Before You Read Lesson 2

Read each statement below. Place a check mark in the circle to indicate whether you agree or disagree with the statement.

	Agree	Disagree
1. Minerals are identified using only their color.	○	○
2. You have used several minerals today.	○	○
3. Most foods except for vegetables contain minerals.	○	○

After You Read Lesson 2

Reread each statement above. If the lesson supports your choice, place a check mark in the *Correct* circle. Then explain how the text supports your choice. If the lesson does not support your choice, place a check mark in the *Incorrect* circle. Then explain why your choice is wrong.

	Correct	Incorrect
1. _____ _____	○	○
2. _____ _____	○	○
3. _____ _____	○	○

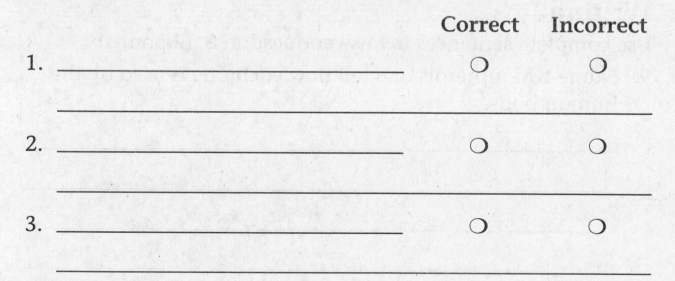

Notes for Home: Your child has completed a pre/post inventory of key concepts in the lesson.
Home Activity: List some minerals, such as copper, quartz, graphite, and iron. Go on a household search for products that contain one or more of these minerals.

Name _____

Reviewing Concepts: Sentence Completion

Complete the sentence with the correct word or phrase.

_____ 1. When a mineral is rubbed on a rough surface, it leaves a _____. (streak, luster)

_____ 2. Pearly, silky, greasy, and dull are ways to describe a mineral's _____. (luster, hardness)

_____ 3. _____ is the hardest mineral. (Talc, Diamond)

_____ 4. Minerals are found in _____ of the things people use every day. (many, few)

_____ 5. _____ is a mineral that helps bones form. (Copper, Calcium)

_____ 6. The mineral fluorite is found in _____. (steel, toothpaste)

_____ 7. The mineral halite is known as _____. (lead, table salt)

_____ 8. Almost _____ foods contain minerals. (all, no)

Writing

Use complete sentences to answer question 9. (2 points)

9. Name two minerals and tell how each one is used by the human body.

_____

_____

_____

_____

Lesson 3: Why is soil important?

Before You Read Lesson 3

Read each statement below. Place a check mark in the circle to indicate whether you agree or disagree with the statement.

	Agree	Disagree
1. Soil is made of decaying plants and animals.	○	○
2. The top layer of soil is called topsoil.	○	○
3. Good soil does not contain living things.	○	○

After You Read Lesson 3

Reread each statement above. If the lesson supports your choice, place a check mark in the *Correct* circle. Then explain how the text supports your choice. If the lesson does not support your choice, place a check mark in the *Incorrect* circle. Then explain why your choice is wrong.

	Correct	Incorrect
1. _____ _____	○	○
2. _____ _____	○	○
3. _____ _____	○	○

Notes for Home: Your child has completed a pre/post inventory of key concepts in the lesson.
Home Activity: Put sand and potting soil into plastic cups. Compare how much water each can hold. Draw a conclusion about which is better for plants.

Name _____

Reviewing Terms: Matching

Match each description with the correct word. Write the letter on the line next to each description.

_____ 1. a thin layer of loose material that covers Earth's land

_____ 2. the process of breaking down the remains of plants and animals

_____ 3. a kind of material released by decay

_____ 4. a soil with a mixture of sand, silt, clay, and humus

a. loam
b. nutrient
c. soil
d. decay

Reviewing Concepts: True or False

Write **T** (True) or **F** (False) on the line before each statement.

_____ 5. It takes about ten years for nature to rebuild lost topsoil.

_____ 6. Topsoil is the bottom layer of soil.

_____ 7. Clay has the smallest soil particle size.

_____ 8. Loam is soil that is good for growing plants.

Applying Concepts: Calculating

9. In a certain area the topsoil is 1.5 meters deep, the subsoil is 3.0 meters deep, and the bedrock is 6.0 meters deep. How many meters deep are all three soil layers together? Show your work. (2 points)

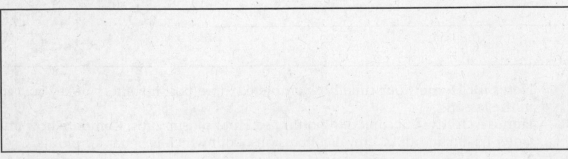

Name _____

Minerals in Foods

Look at the table. A group of students looked at labels on food products at home. They recorded the number of foods they found that contain each mineral on the label.

Mineral	Calcium	Iron	Sodium	Potassium	Copper
Number of foods that have this mineral	32	24	51	12	8

Use the table to answer the questions.

1. Which mineral was found in the most foods?

   _____

2. Which mineral was found in the fewest foods?

   _____

3. The students looked at a total of 60 foods. How many foods in their sample were sodium free?

   _____

4. Which mineral was found in twice as many foods as potassium was found?

   _____

Notes for Home: Your child learned to read a table to compare data.
Home Activity: Help your child make a table showing how much calcium is in different dairy products. Compare which gives the most and least calcium per serving.

Notes

Dear Family,

Your child is learning about two of Earth's important resources. In the science chapter Rocks and Soil, our class has learned about how rocks are made, how rocks are different from one another, what soil is made of, and why soil is important. The children have also learned how and why fossils form in a certain kind of rock, and why minerals are such important materials in people's lives.

As the children learned about rocks and soil, they have also learned many new vocabulary words. Help your child to make these words a part of his or her own vocabulary by using them when you talk together about rocks and soil.

rock
mineral
igneous rock
sedimentary rock
metamorphic rock
soil
decay
nutrient
loam

The following pages include activities that you and your child can do together. By participating in your child's education, you will help to bring the learning home.

© Pearson Education, Inc.

Family Science Activity
Go on a Rock Hunt

Materials:
- sink or bowl with water
- newspaper
- coin

Steps

1. Go outside and look for rocks. Your child should collect at least three rocks to bring home. Help your child find rocks that look different from one another and are easy to carry.

2. Wash the rocks at home to rid them of dirt.

3. Have your child look carefully at each rock. Ask him or her to describe the color(s) in each rock.

4. Have your child describe the texture of each rock—for example, is it smooth or rough? Does the rock have grains or layers in it?

5. Test each rock for the hardness of minerals in it. First, see if each rock easily scratches with a fingernail. Then, test to see if it scratches easily with a coin.

Talk About It

Discuss how the rocks are alike and different. Could any of them be **igneous rocks**—hard rock with grains? Could they be **sedimentary rocks**—softer rocks that form in layers? Could they be **metamorphic**—rocks that changed due to heat and pressure over a long period of time?

Workbook

Vocabulary Puzzle

Circle the five words about soil in the puzzle.

ROCK	SOIL	DECAY
NUTRIENT	LOAM	

```
S  O  A  T  D  E  C  A  Y  P
O  O  N  R  O  E  B  M  E  T
I  O  N  U  T  R  I  E  N  T
L  E  T  A  L  O  A  M  U  S
S  O  I  C  A  C  S  I  G  N
D  E  C  O  K  K  S  O  I  M
```

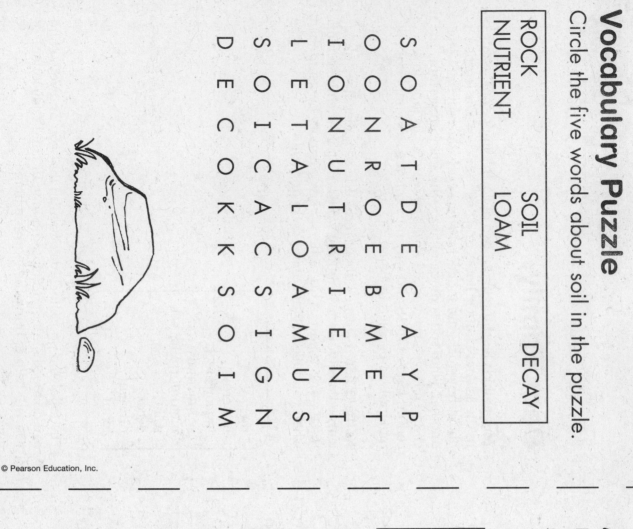

© Pearson Education, Inc.

A Story About Rocks

Use the letter code to spell the words in the story below.

Edwin has a piece of

1. ___ ___ ___ ___ ___ ___ ___ ___ ___ ___ ___ .
       11 4 17 1 11 13 15 14 7 8 2

Sonya has a **2.**

___ ___ ___ ___ ___ ___ .
5 13 16 16 8 10

in

___ ___ ___ ___ ___ ___ .
15 13 2 9

3. ___ ___ ___ ___ ___ ___ ___ ___ ___ ___ ___ ___

16 4 3 8 11 4 12 17 1 15 19

___ ___ ___ ___ .
15 13 2 9

Edwin and Sonya share a **4.**

___ ___ ___ ___ ___ ___ .
11 1 6 12 4

___ . It comes from a **5.**

___ ___ ___ ___ ___ ___ ___ .
11 8 12 4 15 1 10

found in **6.**

___ ___ ___ ___ ___ ___ ___ ___ ___ ___ .
8 6 12 4 13 18 16 15 13 2 9

Workbook

Choose a word to complete each sentence. Underline clues that helped you decide which word to use.

erosion	core	mantle	landforms
crust	lava	magma	weathering

1. The outside layer of Earth, called the _____, is made of rock.

2. Rock in the _____, or middle layer of Earth, is hot enough to flow.

3. Though it is hottest of all, the Earth's inner _____ is packed so tightly that it stays solid.

4. Mountains, hills, valleys, and beaches are examples of Earth's _____.

5. _____ is hot, melted rock that pushes up toward Earth's surface because it is full of gases.

6. When a volcano erupts, melted rock called _____ is forced out.

7. The action of _____ changes a boulder into a pebble over time.

8. Bits of rock can be picked up and carried by wind, water, and glaciers in a process known as _____.

Notes for Home: Your child learned the vocabulary terms for Chapter 8.
Home Activity: Use vocabulary words in sentences that you and your child make up. Then have your child draw pictures to illustrate the words.

Name _____

Sequence

Read the science article.

Growing a Glacier

It takes many years to grow a glacier. First, in a very cold place, snow keeps piling up because it does not melt from year to year. Then top layers press down on lower layers, packing them together. Next, the weight changes bottom layers of snow into ice. Finally, the force is so great it causes the glacier to move over the ground, scraping rocks and dirt as it goes.

© Pearson Education, Inc.

Apply It!

How does a glacier form? Write the steps in order on the graphic organizer.

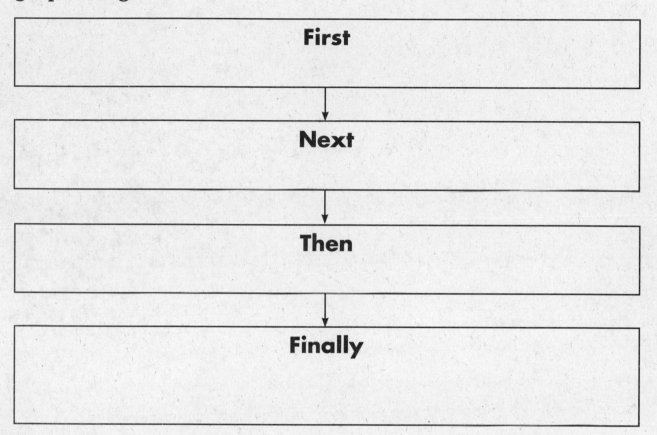

Notes for Home: Your child learned how to sequence events.
Home Activity: Have your child draw a sequence chart showing how forces press on a glacier and cause it to move.

Notes

Lesson 1: What are Earth's layers?

Before You Read Lesson 1

Read each statement below. Place a check mark in the circle to indicate whether you agree or disagree with the statement.

	Agree	Disagree
1. The mantle of Earth moves like soft plastic.	○	○
2. The core of Earth is completely liquid.	○	○
3. A plateau is a high plain.	○	○

After You Read Lesson 1

Reread each statement above. If the lesson supports your choice, place a check mark in the *Correct* circle. Then explain how the text supports your choice. If the lesson does not support your choice, place a check mark in the *Incorrect* circle. Then explain why your choice is wrong.

	Correct	Incorrect
1. _____	○	○
_____		
2. _____	○	○
_____		
3. _____	○	○
_____		

Notes for Home: Your child has completed a pre/post inventory of key concepts in the lesson.
Home Activity: Take a walking tour or look at pictures of local landforms with your child. Discuss how these features might have been shaped by nature.

Reviewing Terms: Sentence Completion

Complete each sentence with the correct word.

_____ 1. The _____ is the outer layer of Earth. (crust, core)

_____ 2. Earth's middle layer is the _____. (core, mantle)

_____ 3. The innermost layer of the Earth is the _____. (crust, core)

_____ 4. _____ are solid features on Earth's crust. (Oceans, Landforms)

Reviewing Concepts: Matching

Match each landform with the correct description. Write the letter on the line next to each description.

_____ 5. a large, mostly flat area   **a.** valley

_____ 6. the land next to the ocean   **b.** plain

_____ 7. a low, narrow area   **c.** coast

_____ 8. a high place   **d.** hill

Writing

Use complete sentences to answer question 9. (2 points)

9. Write a short paragraph that describes Earth's layers.

_____

_____

_____

_____

_____

Lesson 2: What are volcanoes and earthquakes?

Before You Read Lesson 2

Read each statement below. Place a check mark in the circle to indicate whether you agree or disagree with the statement.

	Agree	Disagree
1. Lava hardens to form igneous rock.	○	○
2. Moving parts of Earth's crust cause earthquakes.	○	○
3. Earthquakes often happen along faults.	○	○

After You Read Lesson 2

Reread each statement above. If the lesson supports your choice, place a check mark in the *Correct* circle. Then explain how the text supports your choice. If the lesson does not support your choice, place a check mark in the *Incorrect* circle. Then explain why your choice is wrong.

	Correct	Incorrect
1. _____ _____	○	○
2. _____ _____	○	○
3. _____ _____	○	○

Notes for Home: Your child has completed a pre/post inventory of key concepts in the lesson.
Home Activity: Ask your child to explain how earthquakes and volcanoes are related to the crust and mantle of Earth.

Name _____

Reviewing Terms: Sentence Completion

Complete each sentence with the correct word.

_____ 1. _____ is hot, melted rock under the ground. (Lava, Magma)

_____ 2. Melted rock that has come out of a volcano is called _____. (lava, eruption)

Reviewing Concepts: True or False

Write **T** (True) or **F** (False) on the line before each statement.

_____ 3. Magma forms in Earth's core.

_____ 4. A volcano is an opening in Earth's crust.

_____ 5. When lava cools, it becomes sedimentary rock.

_____ 6. Magma collects underground in magma chambers.

_____ 7. Earthquake vibrations travel as waves.

_____ 8. The farther an earthquake is from a city, the more damage it causes there.

Applying Strategies: Sequence

Use complete sentences to answer question 9. (2 points)

9. Using the clue words in the sentences, write the steps of a volcanic eruption in the correct order.

Next, magma pushes up through cracks in Earth's crust.
First, magma forms deep in the Earth.
Finally, lava cools and hardens, forming igneous rock.
Then magma comes out of the volcano and is called lava.

_____

_____

_____

_____

Lesson 3: What are weathering and erosion?

Before You Read Lesson 3

Read each statement below. Place a check mark in the circle to indicate whether you agree or disagree with the statement.

	Agree	Disagree
1. Erosion is caused solely by wind.	○	○
2. Weathering causes rocks to break up.	○	○
3. Living things do not cause weathering.	○	○

After You Read Lesson 3

Reread each statement above. If the lesson supports your choice, place a check mark in the *Correct* circle. Then explain how the text supports your choice. If the lesson does not support your choice, place a check mark in the *Incorrect* circle. Then explain why your choice is wrong.

	Correct	Incorrect
1. _____	○	○
_____		
2. _____	○	○
_____		
3. _____	○	○
_____		

Notes for Home: Your child has completed a pre/post inventory of key concepts in the lesson.
Home Activity: Freeze an exact amount of water in a measuring cup and then remeasure it. Talk about how the increase in the volume of water when it freezes helps break up rocks.

Reviewing Terms: Matching

Match each description with the correct word. Write the letter on the line next to each description.

_____ 1. any action that breaks rocks into smaller pieces

_____ 2. the movement of broken rocks and Earth materials

a. erosion

b. weathering

Reviewing Concepts: Sentence Completion

Complete the sentence with the correct word or phrase.

_____ 3. Landforms _____ change. (always, never)

_____ 4. Plant's roots can cause _____. (weathering, erosion)

_____ 5. _____ makes water expand and crack rocks. (Freezing, Thawing)

_____ 6. Rainwater causes soil loss by _____. (erosion, gravity)

_____ 7. In dry areas like deserts, _____ causes most of the erosion. (wind, water)

_____ 8. A mudflow is caused by _____. (wind, gravity)

Applying Concepts: Comparing Numbers

9. Using the list below, tell what kind of rock is 10 times larger than a pebble. Explain how you know. (2 points)

<u>Sizes of Rocks</u>

Boulder	300 mm	Cobble	100 mm
Pebble	30 mm	Sand	1 mm

_____

_____

Measuring an Earthquake

The Richter scale measures the strength of earthquakes. Very weak earthquakes have a number from 1 to 3. The strongest earthquakes measure 7 or 8 on the Richter scale.

Richter Magnitude	Effects	Number
Less than 2.0	Not felt	About 8,000 per day
2.0–2.9	Usually not felt	About 1,000 per day
3.0–3.9	Often felt, but rarely causes damage	49,000 per year
4.0–4.9	Not much damage likely	6,200 per year
5.0–5.9	Damage to poorly made buildings over a small area	800 per year
6.0–6.9	Property destroyed over an area up to 100 miles across	120 per year
7.0–7.9	Serious damage over a larger area	18 per year
8.0 or greater	Serious damage in areas several hundred miles across	1 per year

Use the table to answer the questions.

1. About how many earthquakes with a magnitude of 5.0 to 5.9 occur each year? _____

2. What effects can an earthquake with a magnitude of 6.0 to 6.9 have? _____

   _____

3. How would you describe the relationship of the size, or magnitude, of earthquakes and the number of

   earthquakes that occur each year? _____

   _____

Notes for Home: Your child learned how earthquake size and strength are measured.
Home Activity: Talk with your child about any earthquakes in your area. Visit a library or Web site to learn about what to do for safety during an earthquake.

Notes

Dear Family,

Your child is learning about the surface of the earth and ways in which it changes. In the science chapter Changes on Earth, our class has learned about Earth's layers and landforms. The children also learned about events that cause the surface of Earth to change—including volcanoes, earthquakes, weathering, and erosion.

As the children learned about how Earth changes, they have also learned many new vocabulary words. Help your child to make these words a part of his or her own vocabulary by using them when you talk together about Earth and the way in which it changes.

> crust
> mantle
> core
> landform
> magma
> lava
> weathering
> erosion

The following pages include activities that you and your child can do together. By participating in your child's education, you will help to bring the learning home.

Family Science Activity
Create a Landforms Poster

Materials

- old newspapers and magazines
- scissors
- paper
- glue or paste
- marker

Steps

1. With your child, look through old magazines or newspapers. Cut out photographs of scenes in nature. If the photograph has a caption, read it with your child.
2. Have your child point out different landforms in the photographs—such as mountains, plateaus, hills, valleys, lakes, streams, rivers, or oceans.
3. Have your child choose at least four photographs to organize in a poster that shows different landforms.
4. With your child, arrange the photographs on the large sheet of paper. Use the glue or paste to hold the photographs in place. (Leave some space for writing the title and a caption.)
5. Invite your child to write a title and short sentences telling about the photographs in the poster.
6. Ask you child to explain the poster to you. Then, display it in the home.

Vocabulary Riddles

Write the vocabulary word from the box that answers each riddle.

crust	mantle	core	magma

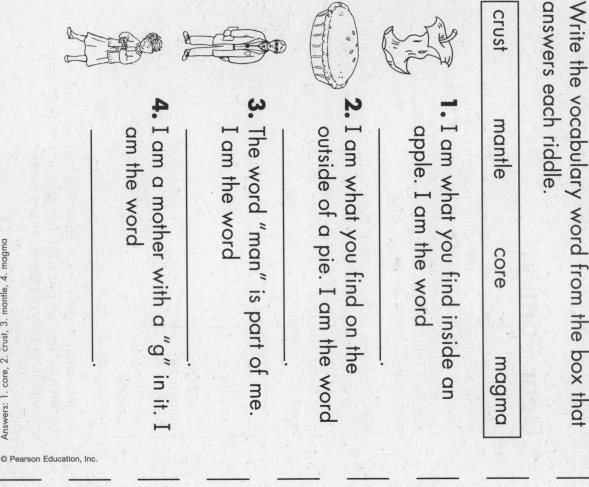

1. I am what you find inside an apple. I am the word

_____

2. I am what you find on the outside of a pie. I am the word

_____

3. The word "man" is part of me. I am the word

_____

4. I am a mother with a "g" in it. I am the word

_____

Word Puzzle

Use the words below to complete the puzzle about Earth. Write one letter in each box.

earthquake	erosion	lava
volcano	weathering	

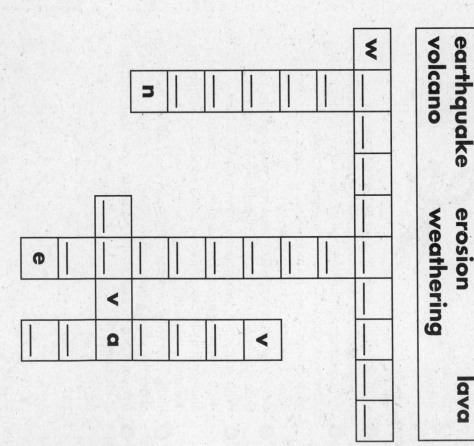

Name _____

Apply It!

Fill in the graphic organizer. Write how solar energy and energy from burning coal are alike and different.

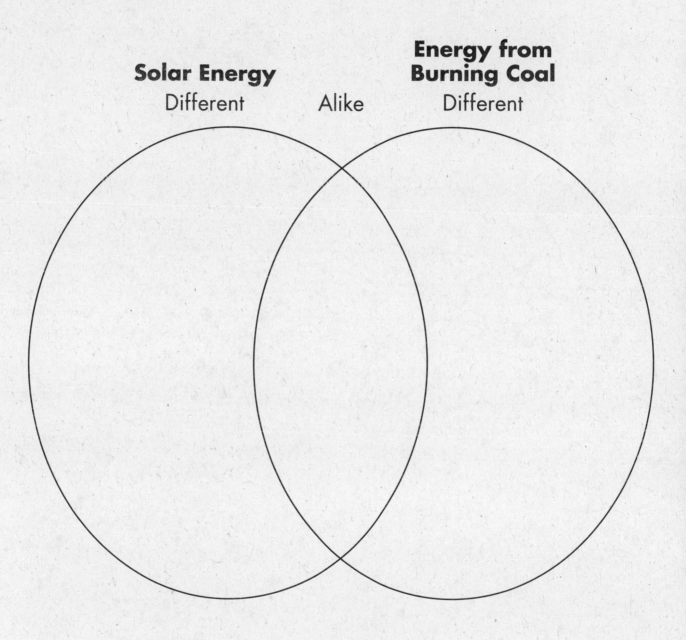

Solar Energy

Different

Alike

Energy from Burning Coal

Different

Notes for Home: Your child learned how to compare and contrast.
Home Activity: With your child, investigate what energy source(s) are used to provide your electricity. How does the power company avoid polluting the air?

© Pearson Education, Inc.

Notes

Name _____

Disappearing Forests

The graph shows how much tropical forest has been lost in just 30 years in three regions of the world as well as in the world overall.

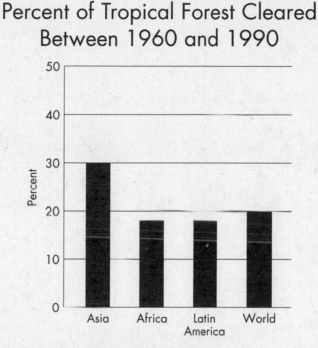

Percent of Tropical Forest Cleared Between 1960 and 1990

Use the graph to answer these questions.

1. What percent of Asia's tropical forests was cut down between 1960 and 1990? _____

2. The bar for *World* shows the average percent of tropical forest cut down in all regions. What percent of the world's tropical forests was cut down between 1960 and 1990?

_____

3. What conclusion can you draw from what this graph shows? _____

_____

_____

Notes for Home: Your child learned to read a bar graph.
Home Activity: Together count the number of food cans, boxes, and packages in your kitchen and make a bar graph that shows this data. Then ask your child questions about the bar graph.

© Pearson Education, Inc.

Notes

Dear Family,

Your child is learning about Earth's natural resources. In the science chapter Natural Resources, our class has learned how we use natural resources—those that can be replaced in a short period of time (**renewable resources**) and those that cannot be replaced (**nonrenewable resources**). The children also learned about conservation and recycling of natural resources.

As the children learned about natural resources, they have also learned many new vocabulary words. Help your child to make these words a part of his or her own vocabulary by using them when you talk together about Earth and its natural resources.

natural resource
renewable resource
nonrenewable resource
conservation
recycle

The following pages include activities that you and your child can do together. By participating in your child's education, you will help to bring the learning home.

Family Science Activity
Recycle a Paper Grocery Bag

Help your child learn how natural resources may be recycled by making a kite from a paper grocery bag.

Materials:

- paper grocery bag
- scissors
- two sticks
- glue or stapler
- spool of string
- yarn or ribbon (optional)

Steps

1. Make a large rectangle from the paper grocery bag. To do this, use scissors to cut around the bottom and then up one side of the bag.

2. Make a diamond shape from the rectangle by folding the ends to a point. Use glue or staples to hold this diamond shape.

3. With the two sticks, form a "t" shape. Tie the "t" shape with a piece of the string.

4. Glue or staple the "t" onto the kite so that the "t" reaches from corner to corner across the diamond shape. (You may also use string to tie the "t" to the four corners of the kite.

5. Tie string from the spool to the center of the "t" with a strong knot. (When you fly the kite, you hold onto the spool and either let out the string or reel it in.)

6. If you like, decorate the kite by attaching pieces of yarn or ribbon that will blow in the breeze when you fly the kite.

Workbook

Recycling

When you **recycle** something, you use a material again to make something else. All the pairs of things below are examples of recycling except for one pair. Circle the one pair that is **not** an example of recycling.

Before Recycling ⟶ **After Recyling**

1. aluminum can ⟶ toy truck

2. newspaper ⟶ envelope

3. rubber tire ⟶ raincoat and boots

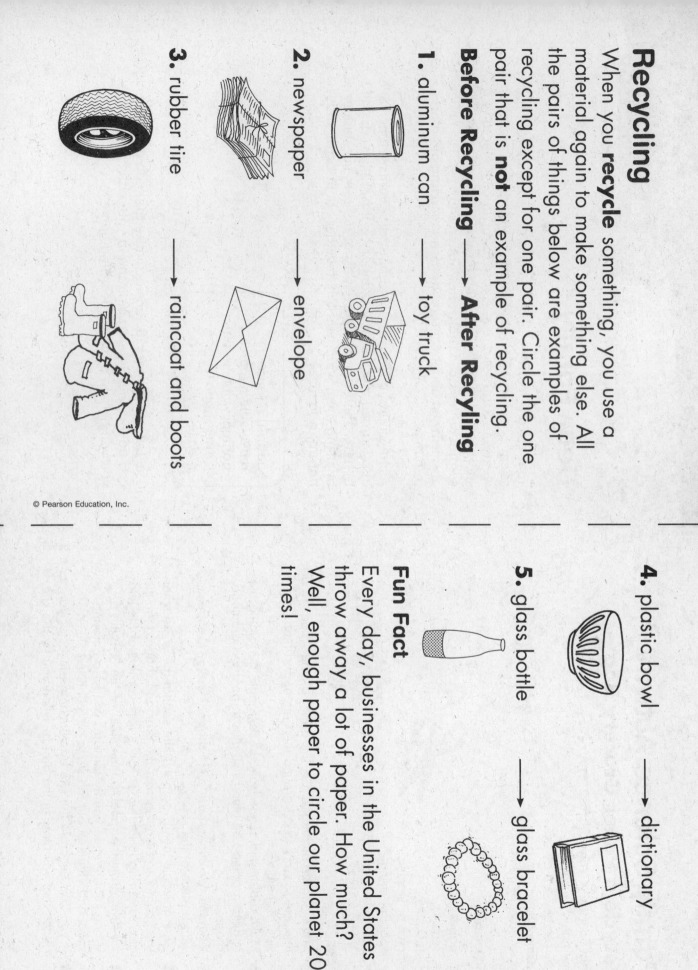

4. plastic bowl ⟶ dictionary

5. glass bottle ⟶ glass bracelet

Fun Fact

Every day, businesses in the United States throw away a lot of paper. How much? Well, enough paper to circle our planet 20 times!

Apply It!

Fill in the graphic organizer. Write three causes and an effect from the article.

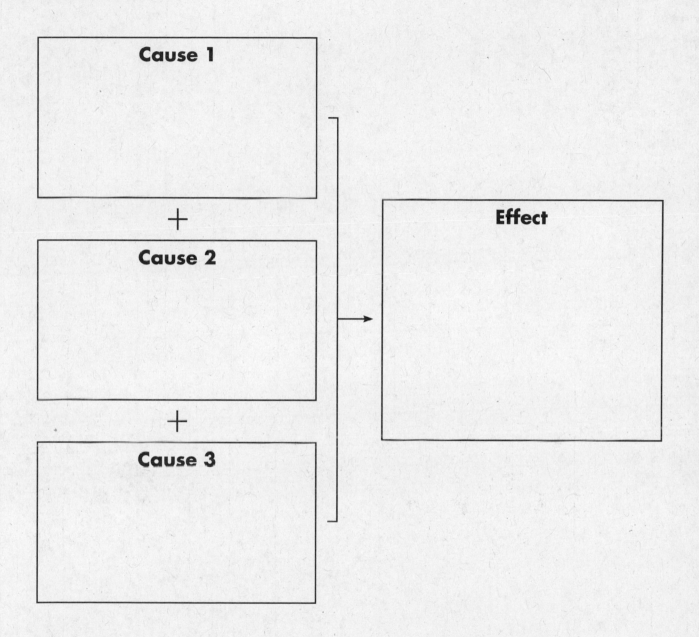

Cause 1

+

Cause 2

+

Cause 3

Effect

© Pearson Education, Inc.

Notes for Home: Your child learned how to identify causes and effects.
Home Activity: With your child, name various things that can change from
a solid to a liquid by adding heat. (Some examples include ice, chocolate, iron,
and gold.)

Notes

Name _____

Write the vocabulary word that answers each riddle.

position	motion	relative position
speed	force	gravity
friction	magnetism	work

1. It tells the location of something. It is specific. Every place on a map has this. What is it? _____

2. It is a force. It opposes motion. It slows moving objects. What is it? _____

3. It is a push or a pull. It can result from two objects coming in contact. It can also result when an object does not touch anything. What is it? _____

4. It locates one thing in relationship to other things. It changes when direction of motion changes. What is it?

   _____

5. It pulls objects toward each other. It is a force. It does not require contact. It increases as mass increases. What is it?

   _____

6. It is a non-contact force that pulls on, or attracts, metals that have iron in them. What is it? _____

7. This tells how fast something changes position. It is a rate of change. It can be fast or slow. It can be constant or variable. What is it? _____

8. You do this when you move something. Machines can help you do this more easily. What is it? _____

9. Anytime an object changes position, this is involved. When your bike rolls, this would be described as forward. When Earth rotates, this is described as circular. What is it?

   _____

Notes for Home: Your child learned the vocabulary terms for Chapter 12.
Home Activity: Ask your child to explain the vocabulary terms to you using photos, diagrams, and other graphics in the chapter to help.

Name _____

⊙ Summarize

Read the science article.

Force

Some forces can cause objects to move without touching them. The force of gravity, for example, pulls a ball that you throw back to Earth. Gravity from the Moon and the Sun tugs at the oceans and causes high and low tides. A magnet also exerts a force. It can pull a metal object to itself from inches, or even feet, away.

Name _____

Apply It!

Fill in the graphic organizer. Write three details and a summary of the article on page 110.

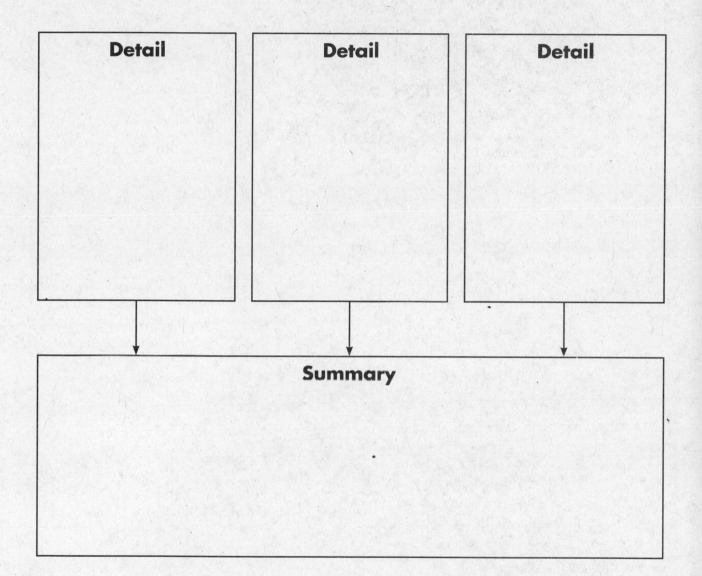

Detail	**Detail**	**Detail**

Summary

Notes for Home: Your child learned how to use details in a summary.
Home Activity: With your child, read an article about something in motion. Together decide what are the important details in the article and summarize them.

Notes

Lesson 1: What happens when things change position?

Before You Read Lesson 1

Read each statement below. Place a check mark in the circle to indicate whether you agree or disagree with the statement.

	Agree	Disagree
1. Motion is change of position.	○	○
2. An object with variable speed moves at the same rate.	○	○
3. A constant speed is always fast.	○	○

After You Read Lesson 1

Reread each statement above. If the lesson supports your choice, place a check mark in the *Correct* circle. Then explain how the text supports your choice. If the lesson does not support your choice, place a check mark in the *Incorrect* circle. Then explain why your choice is wrong.

	Correct	Incorrect
1. _____	○	○
_____		
2. _____	○	○
_____		
3. _____	○	○
_____		

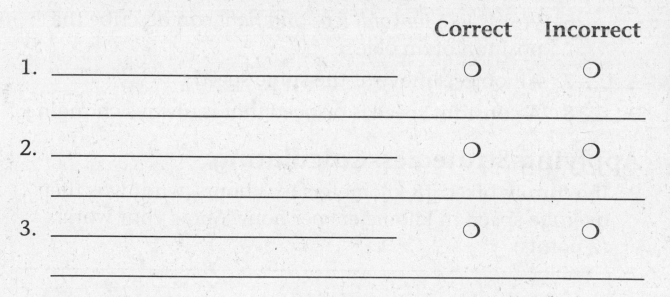

Notes for Home: Your child has completed a pre/post inventory of key concepts in the lesson.
Home Activity: Have your child use toy cars or other movable objects to demonstrate slow, fast, constant, and variable speed.

Reviewing Terms: Sentence Completion

Complete each sentence with the correct word or phrase.

_____ 1. An object's _____ compares its position to the position of other objects. (relative position, speed)

_____ 2. An object that is in _____ keeps changing position. (relative position, motion)

_____ 3. An object's location is its _____. (position, speed)

_____ 4. _____ is how fast an object changes position. (Motion, Speed)

Reviewing Concepts: True or False

Write T (True) or F (False) on the line before each statement.

_____ 5. A map is a drawing of a place that shows the position of objects.

_____ 6. Words like *forward*, *left*, and *right* can describe the position of an object.

_____ 7. All objects move at the same speed.

_____ 8. A constant speed is a speed that is always changing.

Applying Strategies: Calculating

9. If a family biked 18 kilometers in 3 hours, what was their average speed in kilometers per hour? Show your work. (2 points)

Lesson 2: How does force affect motion?

Before You Read Lesson 2

Read each statement below. Place a check mark in the circle to indicate whether you agree or disagree with the statement.

	Agree	Disagree
1. Gravity causes you to have weight.	○	○
2. Friction always helps objects move faster.	○	○
3. Motion is often the result of many forces.	○	○

After You Read Lesson 2

Reread each statement above. If the lesson supports your choice, place a check mark in the *Correct* circle. Then explain how the text supports your choice. If the lesson does not support your choice, place a check mark in the *Incorrect* circle. Then explain why your choice is wrong.

	Correct	Incorrect
1. _____	○	○
_____		
2. _____	○	○
_____		
3. _____	○	○
_____		

Notes for Home: Your child has completed a pre/post inventory of key concepts in the lesson.
Home Activity: Have your child push a toy car or other wheeled object over a wood or tiled floor, then a carpeted floor. Talk about which surface produced more friction.

Reviewing Terms: Matching

Match each description with the correct word. Write the letter on the line next to each description.

_____ 1. any push or pull

_____ 2. a contact force that goes against motion

_____ 3. a non-contact force that pulls all objects together and all objects toward the center of Earth

_____ 4. a non-contact force that pulls on metals with iron in them

a. magnetism
b. force
c. gravity
d. friction

Reviewing Concepts: True or False

Write **T** (True) or **F** (False) on the line before each statement.

_____ 5. Forces can change an object's motion.

_____ 6. Friction can cause a moving object to slow down or to stop.

_____ 7. Equal forces in opposite directions change an object's motion.

_____ 8. Weight is the amount of gravity that pulls on an object.

Applying Strategies: Summarize

Use a complete sentence to answer question 9. (2 points)

9. Write a sentence that summarizes how forces affect motion.

_____

_____

_____

Lesson 3: How do simple machines affect work?

Before You Read Lesson 3

Read each statement below. Place a check mark in the circle to indicate whether you agree or disagree with the statement.

	Agree	Disagree
1. Pushing on a mountain is work.	○	○
2. A wedge is used to split or cut.	○	○
3. A lever rests on a support.	○	○

After You Read Lesson 3

Reread each statement above. If the lesson supports your choice, place a check mark in the *Correct* circle. Then explain how the text supports your choice. If the lesson does not support your choice, place a check mark in the *Incorrect* circle. Then explain why your choice is wrong.

	Correct	Incorrect
1. _____	○	○
2. _____	○	○
3. _____	○	○

© Pearson Education, Inc.

Notes for Home: Your child has completed a pre/post inventory of key concepts in the lesson.
Home Activity: Help your child identify an example of each simple machine among his or her toys or among household objects.

Reviewing Terms: Sentence Completion

Complete the sentence with the correct word.

_____ 1. _____ is done when a force moves an object. (Work, Distance)

Reviewing Concepts: Sentence Completion

Complete each sentence with the correct word or phrase.

_____ 2. Machines _____ change the amount of work needed to do a task. (do, do not)

_____ 3. A ramp is an example of a(n) _____. (pulley, inclined plane)

_____ 4. One example of a _____ is a knife. (wedge, screw)

_____ 5. An inclined plane wrapped around a center post is a _____. (screw, wedge)

_____ 6. A seesaw is one kind of _____. (pulley, lever)

_____ 7. A doorknob is a(n) _____ that makes opening a door easier. (wheel and axle, inclined plane)

_____ 8. You can use a _____ to change the direction of your force. (pulley, wedge)

Writing

Use complete sentences to answer question 9. (2 points)

9. Write a paragraph that tells about a time when you used a simple machine to make work easier.

_____

_____

_____

Relating Speed, Distance, and Time

Use the formulas to solve the word problems.

$$\text{Distance} = \text{Time} \times \text{Speed}$$

$$\text{Time} = \frac{\text{Distance}}{\text{Speed}}$$

$$\text{Speed} = \frac{\text{Distance}}{\text{Time}}$$

To:
Lake Quahanon   4km
Feather Falls   8km
General Store   10km

1. Dennis and Anita rode their bikes an average speed of 8 km per hour. How long did it take them to get to Feather Falls? _____

2. They rode to the General Store and back. It took them 2 hours. How fast did they ride? _____

3. If Dennis and Anita ride to all three places and back, one at a time, and it takes them 4 hours, what was their average speed? _____

Notes for Home: Your child learned to calculate speed, distance, and time.
Home Activity: Walk, drive, or ride with your child to a location whose distance you know. Measure the time it takes. Then calculate your average speed.

Notes

Dear Family,

Your child is learning about forces and motion. In the science chapter Forces and Motion, our class has learned different ways to describe position and motion. We also investigated how forces affect the motion of objects. Students also learned about simple machines and how they help us do work more easily.

Students also learned many new vocabulary words. Help your child to make these words a part of his or her own vocabulary by using them when you talk together about force, motion, and work.

position
motion
relative position
speed
force
friction
gravity
magnetism
work

The following pages include activities that you and your child can do together. By participating in your child's education, you will help to bring the learning home.

Family Science Activity
Slide for Speed

Help your child observe force and motion by noting the speed of different objects as they move down a slide.

Materials:
- Slide
- 2 balls; one ball should be noticeably heavier
- Paper and pencil

Steps

1. Before you go outside, help your child choose two balls. Have your child compare the balls is terms of their size and weight.

2. Go to a park or playground with a slide. Have your child go to the top of the slide and hold each ball, side by side.

3. Direct your child to release both balls. Which one moves faster? Why? Have your child record the results. Repeat the experiment.

4. Have your child draw a picture of your experiment. Have him or her write a few sentences that tell what happened.

Vocabulary Practice

Read the story and underline the vocabulary words wherever they appear.

José said, "Watch me work. My body will be a force that makes this rock move with speed down the hill."

"You can change the position of the rock with your body?" Anna asked.

"Of course," José boasted.

Anna added, "Gravity can also pull a rock down a hill." Anna pulled a magnet out of her backpack. "Magnetism can change the position of a rock, too." Anna placed the magnet by a rock. It turned to the right.

"Wow!" José exclaimed.

Anna smiled and said, "Now, let's see you move that big, big rock all by yourself."

Finding Work

Work is when you use force to move an object. **Look** at the pictures below. **Circle** the pictures that show work being done.

1.

3.

2.

4.

Name _____

Write the words in the blanks.

potential energy	kinetic energy	thermal energy
reflect	refract	absorb
electric charge	electric current	electric circuit

A. Kinds of Energy

_____ _____ (stored)	_____ _____ (moving objects)	_____ _____ (produces heat)	Chemical energy	Electrical energy	Light energy

B. Light Energy—It moves in a straight line until it hits an object.

Light can _____ or bounce.

It can _____ or bend.

It can be _____ or soak in.

C. Electricity

Particles of matter have an _____ _____.

An _____ _____ causes the bulb to light.

Electricity flows through an _____.

Notes for Home: Your child learned the vocabulary terms for Chapter 13.
Home Activity: Ask your child to explain the vocabulary terms to you, using the diagrams and illustrations in their text.

Main Idea and Supporting Details

Read the science article.

Energy in Motion

Energy is always in motion. Look around you and you will see many examples. A bike racing downhill carries energy. Energy moves through wires as electric current. Heat energy moves from a warm object to a cooler object.

Apply It!

Write the main idea of the science article in the box on the next page. Then write details that support the main idea in the circles.

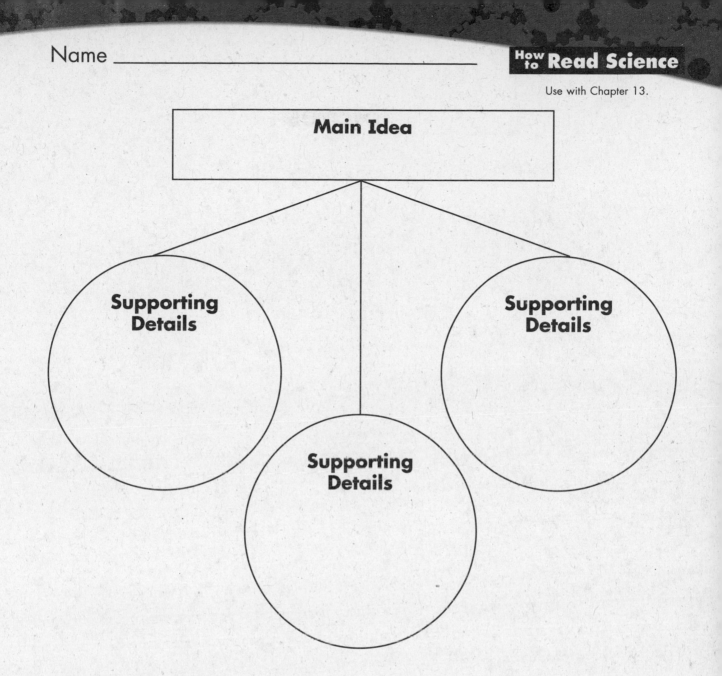

Notes for Home: Your child learned how to identify main ideas and supporting details.
Home Activity: With your child, find and read an article in a magazine. Ask your child to find the main idea of a paragraph in the article and point out supporting details.

Notes

Lesson 1: What is energy?

Before You Read Lesson 1

Read each statement below. Place a check mark in the circle to indicate whether you agree or disagree with the statement.

	Agree	Disagree
1. The Sun gives us heat and light energy.	○	○
2. A pile of coal has potential energy.	○	○
3. A car in the garage has kinetic energy.	○	○

After You Read Lesson 1

Reread each statement above. If the lesson supports your choice, place a check mark in the *Correct* circle. Then explain how the text supports your choice. If the lesson does not support your choice, place a check mark in the *Incorrect* circle. Then explain why your choice is wrong.

	Correct	Incorrect
1. _____ _____	○	○
2. _____ _____	○	○
3. _____ _____	○	○

Notes for Home: Your child has completed a pre/post inventory of key concepts in the lesson.
Home Activity: Have your child help you make a snack. Talk about the forms of potential and kinetic energy involved in the task. Discuss how your body uses the energy.

Reviewing Terms: Matching

Match each description with the correct phrase. Write the letter on the line next to each description.

_____ 1. stored energy

_____ 2. energy of motion

a. potential energy

b. kinetic energy

Reviewing Concepts: True or False

Write **T** (True) or **F** (False) on the line before each statement.

_____ 3. Energy can change form.

_____ 4. Energy is the ability to do work or to cause change.

_____ 5. There is one form of energy.

_____ 6. Fuels store kinetic energy.

_____ 7. Chemical energy can be stored in batteries.

_____ 8. Potential energy can change to kinetic energy.

Writing

Use complete sentences to answer question 9. (2 points)

9. Describe one example of potential energy and one example of kinetic energy with which you are familiar.

_____

_____

_____

_____

Lesson 2: How does energy change form?

Before You Read Lesson 2

Read each statement below. Place a check mark in the circle to indicate whether you agree or disagree with the statement.

	Agree	Disagree
1. A carrot holds chemical energy.	○	○
2. Electrical charges give off heat.	○	○
3. Energy is often useful when it is changing form.	○	○

After You Read Lesson 2

Reread each statement above. If the lesson supports your choice, place a check mark in the *Correct* circle. Then explain how the text supports your choice. If the lesson does not support your choice, place a check mark in the *Incorrect* circle. Then explain why your choice is wrong.

	Correct	Incorrect
1. _____	○	○
_____		
2. _____	○	○
_____		
3. _____	○	○
_____		

Notes for Home: Your child has completed a pre/post inventory of key concepts in the lesson.
Home Activity: With your child, make waves using a spiral wire toy. Identify the trough and crest. Note how the waves change as you add more energy with your arms.

Name _____

Reviewing Concepts: Sentence Completion

Complete each sentence with the correct word.

_____ 1. Your body uses the _____ energy in food. (electrical, chemical)

_____ 2. When energy changes form, some energy is always given off as _____. (heat, light)

_____ 3. The energy in moving objects is _____ energy. (thermal, mechanical)

_____ 4. The appliances in people's homes are powered by _____ energy. (electrical, light)

_____ 5. Plants use _____ energy from the Sun to make food. (chemical, light)

_____ 6. Waves carry _____. (water, energy)

_____ 7. As waves move away from their source, they _____ energy. (gain, lose)

_____ 8. Waves that are _____ have lots of energy. (wide, narrow)

Writing

Use complete sentences to answer question 9. (2 points)

9. Write a paragraph that describes energy changing from one form to another.

_____

_____

_____

_____

Lesson 3: What is heat energy?

Before You Read Lesson 3

Read each statement below. Place a check mark in the circle to indicate whether you agree or disagree with the statement.

	Agree	Disagree
1. Thermal energy comes from the motion of particles.	○	○
2. Heat travels from cooler to warmer matter.	○	○
3. Heat can change the state of matter.	○	○

After You Read Lesson 3

Reread each statement above. If the lesson supports your choice, place a check mark in the *Correct* circle. Then explain how the text supports your choice. If the lesson does not support your choice, place a check mark in the *Incorrect* circle. Then explain why your choice is wrong.

	Correct	Incorrect
1. _____ _____	○	○
2. _____ _____	○	○
3. _____ _____	○	○

Notes for Home: Your child has completed a pre/post inventory of key concepts in the lesson.
Home Activity: With your child, make juice pops in an ice tray. Discuss why heat moved from the liquid juice into the freezer and what changed because of the loss.

Name _____

Reviewing Terms: Sentence Completion

Complete the sentence with the correct phrase.

_____ 1. The energy of moving particles is _____.
(thermal energy, electrical energy)

Reviewing Concepts: True or False

Write **T** (True) or **F** (False) on the line before each statement.

_____ 2. Thermal energy travels as heat.

_____ 3. Heat moves from cooler objects to warmer objects.

_____ 4. When energy changes form, some heat is given off.

_____ 5. The change from ice to liquid water is related to a change in energy.

_____ 6. Friction caused by rubbing gives off heat.

_____ 7. Heat can cause water to evaporate.

_____ 8. Liquid water boils as it turns to ice.

Applying Strategies: Calculating

9. On the Fahrenheit scale, water boils at 212 degrees and freezes at 32 degrees. What is the difference between these two temperatures? Show your work. (2 points)

Name _____

Lesson 4: What is light energy?

Before You Read Lesson 4

Read each statement below. Place a check mark in the circle to indicate whether you agree or disagree with the statement.

	Agree	Disagree
1. Only the Sun and chemical changes produce light.	○	○
2. Reflected light bounces off a smooth surface.	○	○
3. Color results from refracted light.	○	○

After You Read Lesson 4

Reread each statement above. If the lesson supports your choice, place a check mark in the *Correct* circle. Then explain how the text supports your choice. If the lesson does not support your choice, place a check mark in the *Incorrect* circle. Then explain why your choice is wrong.

	Correct	Incorrect
1. _____ _____	○	○
2. _____ _____	○	○
3. _____ _____	○	○

Notes for Home: Your child has completed a pre/post inventory of key concepts in the lesson.
Home Activity: With your child, place a black cloth and a white cloth in sunlight. Discuss why the black cloth absorbs more heat than the white cloth.

Reviewing Terms: Matching

Match each description with the correct word or phrase. Write the letter on the line next to each description.

_____ 1. light bouncing off an object

_____ 2. light bending

_____ 3. light being taken in by an object

a. absorb

b. reflect

c. refract

Reviewing Concepts: Sentence Completion

Complete each sentence with the correct word or phrase.

_____ 4. _____ is energy that can be seen. (Light, Heat)

_____ 5. Light bulbs use _____ to make light. (electrical energy, chemical energy)

_____ 6. Light travels from its source in _____. (straight lines, curved lines)

_____ 7. The length of a shadow depends on the _____ of the light. (brightness, angle)

_____ 8. Light is made up of _____ colors. (one, many)

Applying Strategies: Main Idea and Supporting Details

Use complete sentences to answer question 9. (2 points)

9. List three details that support the main idea below.

Main Idea: Objects can reflect, refract, or absorb light.

Detail: _____

Detail: _____

Detail: _____

_____

Lesson 5: What is electrical energy?

Before You Read Lesson 5

Read each statement below. Place a check mark in the circle to indicate whether you agree or disagree with the statement.

	Agree	Disagree
1. Lightning is a kind of electric circuit.	○	○
2. Electric energy can be changed to sound energy.	○	○
3. An open switch breaks an electric circuit.	○	○

After You Read Lesson 5

Reread each statement above. If the lesson supports your choice, place a check mark in the *Correct* circle. Then explain how the text supports your choice. If the lesson does not support your choice, place a check mark in the *Incorrect* circle. Then explain why your choice is wrong.

	Correct	Incorrect
1. _____ _____	○	○
2. _____ _____	○	○
3. _____ _____	○	○

Notes for Home: Your child has completed a pre/post inventory of key concepts in the lesson.
Home Activity: With your child, list appliances in your home that use electricity. Make a chart to sort the appliances into those used to produce light, heat, and sound.

Name _____

Reviewing Terms: Matching

Match each description with the correct phrase. Write the letter on the line next to each description.

_____ 1. a tiny amount of energy, this can be positive or negative

_____ 2. movement of electrical energy or electrical charge

_____ 3. the path through which an electric current flows

a. electric circuit
b. electric charge
c. electric current

Reviewing Concepts: True or False

Write **T** (True) or **F** (False) on the line before each statement.

_____ 4. Particles balance each other when they have an equal number of positive and negative charges.

_____ 5. Two objects with negative charges will attract each other.

_____ 6. Lightning is an uncontrolled electric current.

_____ 7. When the switch in an electric circuit is open, current can flow.

_____ 8. Electrical energy is changed to sound energy in a radio speaker.

Applying Strategies: Compare and Contrast

Use complete sentences to answer question 9. (2 points)

9. Describe one similarity and one difference between the electricity in lightning and the electricity in an electrical circuit.

_____

_____

_____

_____

Name _____

Measuring Temperature

Mickie used the thermometer below to measure the
temperatures of tap water and bath water.

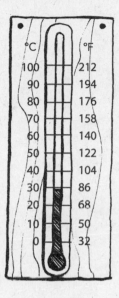

Use the thermometer to answer the questions. Place a ruler to
help you compare degrees Celsius and degrees Fahrenheit.

1. Mickie found that her bath water was 120°F. About how
   many degrees Celsius is this? _____

2. The water from the tap was about 18°C. Which of
   the following is closest to this temperature in degrees
   Fahrenheit?

   A. 30°F   **B.** 45°F   **C.** 60°F   **D.** 75°F

   _____

3. Mickie took her temperature. It was 37°C. Normal body
   temperature in degrees Fahrenheit is 98.6. Did Mickie have
   a fever? How do you know? _____

   _____

Notes for Home: Your child measured temperature in degrees Fahrenheit
and Celsius.
Home Activity: Help your child measure his or her temperature in degrees
Fahrenheit and convert this to degrees Celsius. (Use the formula $F = (C \times 9/5) + 32$ to check the estimate.)

Notes

Dear Family,

Your child is learning about the many forms of energy we use every day, from the chemical energy stored in food and fuel to the kinetic energy of a moving object. In the chapter Energy, we also explored electrical energy, light energy, and thermal energy. Your child studied how energy can change forms. For example, a hair dryer turns electricity into heat, sound, and kinetic energy.

Your child learned many new vocabulary words in this chapter. Help your child to make these words a part of his or her own vocabulary by using them when you talk together about energy.

potential energy
kinetic energy
thermal energy
reflect
refract
absorb
electric charge
electric current
electric circuit

The following pages include activities that you and your child can do together. By participating in your child's education, you will help to bring the learning home.

Family Science Activity
Energy Watch

Use this chart to keep a family energy survey. Write an example of the five forms of energy you use every day. Energy is a part of every movement we make, so you won't be able to include every example. Choose interesting examples and talk about how this energy was useful in your activities.

Chemical	Kinetic	Electrical	Light	Thermal

Talk About It

Which form of energy do you think you use the most every day? Why? What would your life be like without electricity? Make a list of your habits and hobbies that would have to change.

Workbook

Vocabulary Practice: Energy

Write a vocabulary word to answer each clue. The shaded letters will spell the answer to the question on the next page. You can see a list of the vocabulary words on page 1 of the booklet.

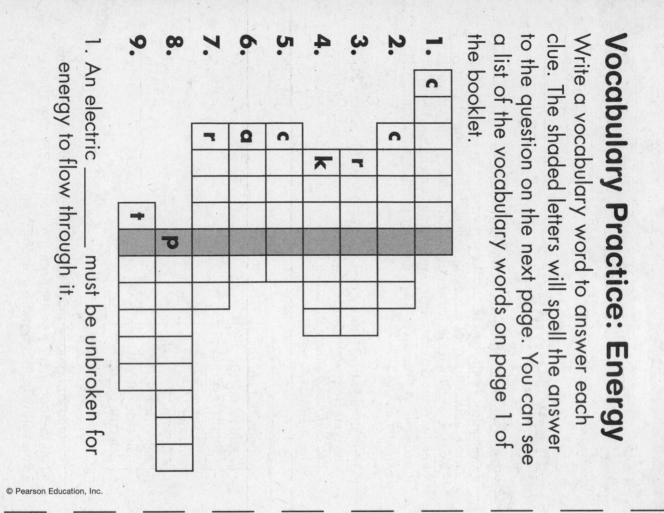

1. [c]
2. [c]
3. [r] [k]
4.
5. [c] [a]
6. [r] [p]
7.
8. [t]
9.

1. An electric _____ must be unbroken for energy to flow through it.

© Pearson Education, Inc.

2. Electric _____ is the movement of electrical energy from one place to another.

3. A mirror will _____ light when it bounces the light back to your eyes.

4. The energy of motion is _____ energy.

5. An electric _____ is a tiny amount of energy.

6. If an object looks black, it will _____ all the colors of sunlight.

7. Light rays bend when they _____.

8. Stored energy is _____ energy.

9. The energy of moving particles is _____ energy.

What invention by Samuel Morse sends messages by making and breaking an electric circuit?

Fun Fact

Calories measure the energy stored in food. When you look at the calorie content of any food, you are looking at how much energy the food could give your body.

Name _____

Write a vocabulary term from the word bank to complete each sentence. Underline the clues that helped you decide which vocabulary term to write.

pitch	vibration	compression wave

1. Energy causes particles of matter to move back and forth. It is this _____ that produces sound.

2. Wave motion involves passing energy through particles. Some particles are squeezed together while others are spread apart. This is called a _____.

3. A bass string vibrates slowly and produces a low sound. A violin string vibrates quickly and produces a high sound. This is a difference in _____.

Explain what is happening in the picture. Write three sentences. Use a vocabulary word in each sentence.

4. _____

5. _____

6. _____

Notes for Home: Your child learned the vocabulary terms for Chapter 14.
Home Activity: Ask your child to demonstrate or illustrate the meaning of each vocabulary term as he or she explains it to you.

⌖ Compare and Contrast

Read the paragraph.

Musical Instruments

A trombone and a bassoon are both wind instruments. This means they make sounds when you cause the air in them to vibrate. A trombonist vibrates his or her lips and blows into the trombone mouthpiece. This makes the air inside the instrument vibrate. A bassoonist blows on a reed, or a thin piece of wood. This makes the air in the bassoon vibrate.

Apply It!

Fill in the graphic organizer. Write ways the trombone and the bassoon are alike and ways they are different.

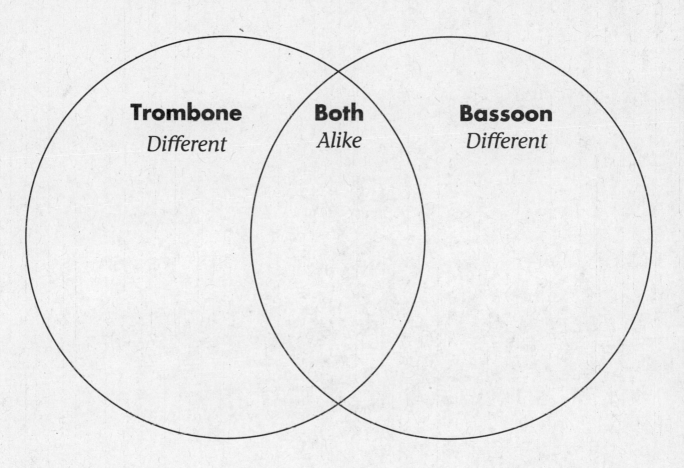

Trombone
Different

Both
Alike

Bassoon
Different

Notes for Home: Your child learned how to compare and contrast objects.
Home Activity: With your child, listen to a recording of music. Identify several instruments. Discuss how their sounds are different and how they might be produced.

Notes

Lesson 1: What causes sounds?

Before You Read Lesson 1

Read each statement below. Place a check mark in the circle to indicate whether you agree or disagree with the statement.

	Agree	Disagree
1. When you speak, your vocal chords vibrate.	◯	◯
2. Pitch is loudness or softness of sound.	◯	◯
3. Short, thin harp strings make high sounds.	◯	◯

After You Read Lesson 1

Reread each statement above. If the lesson supports your choice, place a check mark in the *Correct* circle. Then explain how the text supports your choice. If the lesson does not support your choice, place a check mark in the *Incorrect* circle. Then explain why your choice is wrong.

	Correct	Incorrect
1. _____	◯	◯
_____		
2. _____	◯	◯
_____		
3. _____	◯	◯
_____		

Notes for Home: Your child has completed a pre/post inventory of key concepts in the lesson.
Home Activity: Have your child experiment with pitch and loudness by strumming stretched rubber bands with a finger and tapping glasses with a spoon.

Reviewing Terms: Matching

Match each description with the correct word or phrase. Write the letter on the line next to each description.

_____ 1. a back-and-forth motion

_____ 2. how high or low a sound is

a. pitch

b. vibration

Reviewing Concepts: Sentence Completion

Complete each sentence with the correct word.

_____ 3. _____ only happens when matter vibrates. (Sound, Light)

_____ 4. Objects that vibrate slowly make a sound with a _____ pitch. (high, low)

_____ 5. The _____ of sound depends on the strength of the vibrations. (pitch, loudness)

_____ 6. The harder you hit a drum, the _____ the sound. (louder, higher)

_____ 7. Wind instruments make sounds when _____ inside them vibrates. (string, air)

_____ 8. When people _____, their vocal chords vibrate. (speak, hear)

Applying Strategies: Compare and Contrast

Use complete sentences to answer question 9. (2 points)

9. Name one similarity and one difference between *pitch* and *loudness*.

_____

_____

_____

Lesson 2: How does sound travel?

Before You Read Lesson 2

Read each statement below. Place a check mark in the circle to indicate whether you agree or disagree with the statement.

	Agree	Disagree
1. Without matter there is no sound.	○	○
2. Sound travels in compression waves.	○	○
3. Sound cannot travel through gases.	○	○

After You Read Lesson 2

Reread each statement above. If the lesson supports your choice, place a check mark in the *Correct* circle. Then explain how the text supports your choice. If the lesson does not support your choice, place a check mark in the *Incorrect* circle. Then explain why your choice is wrong.

	Correct	Incorrect
1. _____ _____	○	○
2. _____ _____	○	○
3. _____ _____	○	○

Notes for Home: Your child has completed a pre/post inventory of key concepts in the lesson.
Home Activity: Have your child listen to a sound traveling through air, then through water, for example, in a bathtub.

Reviewing Terms: Sentence Completion

Complete the sentence with the correct word.

_____ 1. Sound waves are examples of
_____ waves. (compression,
atmospheric)

Reviewing Concepts: True or False

Write **T** (True) or **F** (False) on the line before each statement.

_____ 2. Sound travels in matter.

_____ 3. Sound cannot travel in outer space.

_____ 4. Sound travels through solids, but not through
liquids and gases.

_____ 5. Echoes are caused when sound waves are absorbed
by an object.

_____ 6. The outer ear collects sound waves traveling in
the air.

_____ 7. Humans and animals can all hear the same sounds.

_____ 8. Bats use sound to find food.

Applying Strategies: Converting Units

9. The speed of sound in steel is 5,200 meters per second.
Write this speed using the unit kilometers per second.
Remember that 1,000 meters = 1 kilometer. Show your
work. (2 points)

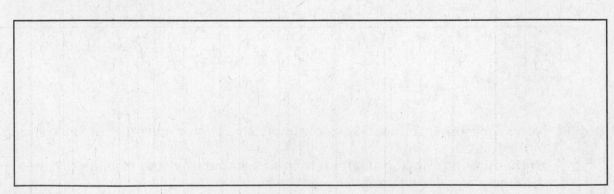

Comparing Speeds of Sound

Compare the speeds at which sound travels through the materials in the table. Use the data to answer the questions.

Materials	Speed (Meters Per Second)
Rubber	60
Cork	500
Lead	1,210
Water at 25° Celsius	1,496
Sea water at 25° Celsius	1,531
Brick	3,650
Glass	4,540
Aluminum	5,000
Stone	5,971

1. What solids carry sound slower than water carries it?

   _____

2. Does sound travel faster through fresh water or

   salt water? _____

3. Suppose an earthquake occurs in the ocean floor. What different materials will its sound travel through? How fast

   will it travel through each material? _____

   _____

   _____

Notes for Home: Your child compared the speeds at which sound travels through different materials.
Home Activity: Discuss with your child how the particles of the different materials in the chart might differ and how these differences affect their ability to transmit sound waves.

Notes

Dear Family,

Your child is learning how different sounds are produced. In the science chapter Sound, our class learned how sound travels. Students studied how humans produce sounds and how they hear. Our class also learned how certain musical instruments produce sounds.

In addition to learning how sound travels through different materials, students learned many new vocabulary words. Help your child to make these words a part of his or her own vocabulary by using them when you talk together about sound.

vibration
pitch
compression wave

The following pages include activities that you and your child can do together. By participating in your child's education, you will help to bring the learning home.

Family Science Activity
Sound Mysteries

Materials:

- piles of items, such as popcorn kernels, pennies, grains of rice, paper clips, pebbles, soil, or sand (NOTE: The piles should be similar in size.)
- four opaque plastic cups
- aluminum paper squares
- paper or pencil

Steps

1. Show your child each pile of items. Then, have your child leave the room while you place each item into a plastic cup. Place a foil square over each cups opening.
2. Invite your child to return to the room. Remove one cup's cover; place your hand over the top of the cup. Make sure your child cannot see what is inside the cup.
3. Shake the cup. Ask your child which of the four objects he or she heard rattle inside the cup. Have your child write Cup 1 and the name of the object on a piece of paper.
4. Return the cup to the table and cover it. Repeat Step 3 with Cups 2, 3, and 4.
5. Remove each cup's cover. Compare your child's guesses to the actual content in each cup.

Vocabulary Practice

Find a vocabulary word in each list of letters.
Circle the letters of the word. Write the word
on the line.

Word Bank

| vibration | pitch | compression wave |

d h a p i w z y d x w t c h d i f t u x d

_____

p c o m e i p r e s s r i o n t n w a v e x

_____

s a d f q v i o b r a w l t i o n f w z b h d q

_____

Answer with an Antonym

Antonyms are words that have the opposite
meaning of another word. Draw a line
from a word about sound on the left to its
antonym on the right.

1. to vibrate   silence

2. high   low

3. sound   soft

4. loud   to be still

5. receive   send

Fun Fact

Did you ever see a dog prick up its ears
and turn them toward a sound? Dogs move
their ears in order to hear well. A dog uses
more than eighteen different muscles to tilt,
raise, or turn its ears.

Name _____

Read each sentence. Choose the answer that gives the best meaning for the boldface word.

1. Earth makes a complete **rotation** every twenty-four hours.
   A. circle   B. spin   C. day   D. week

2. The Sun is a **star** that gives Earth heat and light.
   A. super-sized planet   C. very distant object
   B. huge rock   D. hot ball of gases

3. A full Moon and a crescent Moon are two Moon **phases**.
   A. stages   C. craters
   B. separate parts   D. copies

4. Earth spins on its **axis** like a wheel spins on an axle.
   A. east-to-west line   C. line from pole to pole
   B. flat pancake shape   D. force field that pulls

5. In a year, Earth makes one **revolution** around the Sun.
   A. circle around a center   C. set of seasons
   B. trip to and from   D. change of direction

6. In a **lunar eclipse**, Earth moves between the Sun and Moon.
   A. blocking of the Sun's light
   B. Earth's shadow covering Moon
   C. blocking of the Moon by Earth
   D. Moon's shadow covering Earth

7. A **telescope** shows details of the Moon and stars.
   A. tool that magnifies   C. lighted tube
   B. tool that makes   D. darkened pipe
   things look smaller

8. Long ago, people named each **constellation** of stars.
   A. any cluster of stars   C. group of stars in a pattern
   B. quarter of the sky   D. half of the sky

Notes for Home: Your child learned the vocabulary terms for Chapter 15.
Home Activity: Ask your child to find an example or diagram in the chapter to help explain the meaning of each vocabulary word.

Sequence

Study the set of diagrams that show a pattern.

Apply It!

In the box below, draw a diagram of what will happen next in the pattern. Show the shadow that will appear and its direction.

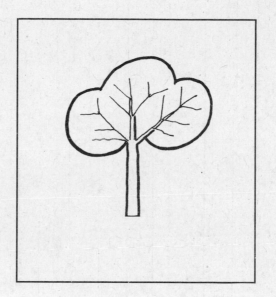

Notes for Home: Your child learned how to use a diagrammed sequence to predict what will happen next.
Home Activity: With your child, use a flashlight and an object to make shadows. Describe the sequence of movements that makes the shadow lengthen.

Notes

Lesson 1: What are some patterns that repeat every day?

Before You Read Lesson 1

Read each statement below. Place a check mark in the circle to indicate whether you agree or disagree with the statement.

	Agree	Disagree
1. Earth's rotation causes day and night.	○	○
2. Earth rotates faster in winter.	○	○
3. Shadows fall to the east in the morning.	○	○

After You Read Lesson 1

Reread each statement above. If the lesson supports your choice, place a check mark in the *Correct* circle. Then explain how the text supports your choice. If the lesson does not support your choice, place a check mark in the *Incorrect* circle. Then explain why your choice is wrong.

	Correct	Incorrect
1. _____ _____	○	○
2. _____ _____	○	○
3. _____ _____	○	○

Notes for Home: Your child has completed a pre/post inventory of key concepts in the lesson.
Home Activity: Have your child use a ball or globe to model Earth's rotation while you hold a flashlight. Discuss how rotation causes day and night.

© Pearson Education, Inc.

Reviewing Terms: Matching

Match each description with the correct word. Write the letter on the line next to each description.

_____ 1. a giant ball of hot, glowing gases
_____ 2. the imaginary line around which Earth spins
_____ 3. one complete spin on an axis

a. axis
b. star
c. rotation

Reviewing Concepts: Sentence Completion

Complete each sentence with the correct word or phrase.

_____ 4. Earth is _____ compared to the Sun. (large, small)

_____ 5. At any time, _____ of Earth is facing the Sun. (half, all)

_____ 6. Earth makes one rotation every _____ hours. (12, 24)

_____ 7. The length and direction of shadows _____ throughout the day. (change, stay the same)

_____ 8. Shadows are very _____ at midday. (long, short)

Applying Strategies: Sequence

9. The Sun's place in the sky seems to change throughout the day. The steps are listed below, but they are out of order. Use the clue words to place the steps in the correct order. (2 points)

Finally, the Sun appears to set in the west.
First, the Sun appears to rise in the east.
Next, the Sun appears to move across the sky.

_____

_____

_____

Lesson 2: What patterns repeat every year?

Before You Read Lesson 2

Read each statement below. Place a check mark in the circle to indicate whether you agree or disagree with the statement.

	Agree	Disagree
1. A revolution is one complete spin.	O	O
2. December is summer time in the southern half of Earth.	O	O
3. We have less sunlight in winter.	O	O

After You Read Lesson 2

Reread each statement above. If the lesson supports your choice, place a check mark in the *Correct* circle. Then explain how the text supports your choice. If the lesson does not support your choice, place a check mark in the *Incorrect* circle. Then explain why your choice is wrong.

	Correct	Incorrect
1. _____	O	O
_____		
2. _____	O	O
_____		
3. _____	O	O
_____		

Notes for Home: Your child has completed a pre/post inventory of key concepts in the lesson.
Home Activity: With your child, use a flashlight and a ball held at a tilted angle to model direct and indirect rays of light hitting a sphere.

Reviewing Terms: Sentence Completion
Complete the sentence with the correct word.

_____ 1. A _____ is one complete trip around the Sun.
(revolution, rotation)

Reviewing Concepts: True or False
Write **T** (True) or **F** (False) on the line before each statement.

_____ 2. Earth's axis always points toward the same direction in space.

_____ 3. The places on Earth that receive the most direct Sun are the warmest.

_____ 4. The seasons are caused by Earth's tilt and movement around the Sun.

_____ 5. Earth makes one revolution in 24 hours.

_____ 6. In most places on Earth the number of hours of daylight and darkness changes throughout the year.

_____ 7. During winter there are more hours of daylight than darkness.

_____ 8. The Sun appears higher in the sky during summer than it does in winter.

Applying Strategies: Calculating
9. In the Northern United States there are 15 hours of daylight on some days during June. On those days, how many hours of darkness are there? Show your work, and write a sentence that explains how you found your answer. (2 points)

_____

_____

_____

Workbook

Name _____

Lesson 3: Why does the Moon's shape change?

Before You Read Lesson 3

Read each statement below. Place a check mark in the circle to indicate whether you agree or disagree with the statement.

	Agree	Disagree
1. The Moon reflects sunlight.	○	○
2. The Moon changes shape each month.	○	○
3. The Moon repeats four phases each $29\frac{1}{2}$ days.	○	○

After You Read Lesson 3

Reread each statement above. If the lesson supports your choice, place a check mark in the *Correct* circle. Then explain how the text supports your choice. If the lesson does not support your choice, place a check mark in the *Incorrect* circle. Then explain why your choice is wrong.

	Correct	Incorrect
1. _____	○	○
_____		
2. _____	○	○
_____		
3. _____	○	○
_____		

Notes for Home: Your child has completed a pre/post inventory of key concepts in the lesson.
Home Activity: With your child, observe the Moon, draw it, and identify its phase. Observe and sketch it again several days later and compare how it looks.

Reviewing Terms: Matching

Match each description with the correct word or phrase. Write the letter on the line next to each description.

_____ 1. each different way the Moon looks

_____ 2. when Earth blocks sunlight from reaching the Moon

a. lunar eclipse

b. phase

Reviewing Concepts: True or False

Write **T** (True) or **F** (False) on the line before each statement.

_____ 3. It takes the Moon about 29 days to complete one rotation.

_____ 4. The Moon makes its own light.

_____ 5. During a New Moon, the Moon looks like a half circle.

_____ 6. The Moon looks like a half circle during the First Quarter Moon.

_____ 7. The Full Moon looks like a circle.

_____ 8. The lighted half of the Moon can always be seen from Earth.

Writing

9. Write a paragraph that describes the positions of the Earth, Moon, and Sun during a lunar eclipse. (2 points)

_____

_____

_____

_____

Lesson 4: What are star patterns?

Before You Read Lesson 4

Read each statement below. Place a check mark in the circle to indicate whether you agree or disagree with the statement.

	Agree	Disagree
1. Stars in a constellation make a pattern.	○	○
2. Most stars can be seen with the eyes alone.	○	○
3. Stars are moving in space.	○	○

After You Read Lesson 4

Reread each statement above. If the lesson supports your choice, place a check mark in the *Correct* circle. Then explain how the text supports your choice. If the lesson does not support your choice, place a check mark in the *Incorrect* circle. Then explain why your choice is wrong.

	Correct	Incorrect
1. _____ _____	○	○
2. _____ _____	○	○
3. _____ _____	○	○

Notes for Home: Your child has completed a pre/post inventory of key concepts in the lesson.
Home Activity: With your child, locate an outdoor space to view stars at night. (If possible, find a location that is not brightly lit.) Look for a constellation.

Reviewing Terms: Matching

Match each description with the correct word. Write the letter on the line next to each description.

_____ 1. a group of stars that makes a pattern

_____ 2. a tool that magnifies faraway objects

a. telescope

b. constellation

Reviewing Concepts: True or False

Write **T** (True) or **F** (False) on the line before each statement.

_____ 3. All stars are the same size.

_____ 4. Some stars are brighter than others.

_____ 5. Some telescopes use mirrors and lenses.

_____ 6. The stars in constellations are close together in space.

_____ 7. Stars appear to move across the sky at night.

_____ 8. Constellations always appear in the same part of the sky.

Applying Strategies: Main Idea and Supporting Details

Use complete sentences to answer question 9. (2 points)

9. Write three details that support the main idea given below.
   Main Idea: Stars appear in patterns in the sky.

Detail: _____

Detail: _____

Detail: _____

Name _____

Comparing Times of Moonrise and Moonset

Like the Sun, the Moon rises and sets every day. However, the time of moonrise and moonset varies more than sunrise and sunset do. Use the table below to answer the questions.

DATE	MOONRISE	MOONSET
May 9, 2004	1:00 A.M.	9:48 A.M.
July 9, 2004	12:28 A.M.	1:34 P.M.
September 9, 2004	12:55 A.M.	5:04 P.M.
November 9, 2004	2:59 A.M.	3:09 P.M.

1. How many hours and minutes were between moonrise and moonset on May 9?

   _____

2. Which date had the longest time between moonrise and moonset?

   _____

3. If you stayed up to see the Moon rise, on which date would you stay up the longest?

   _____

4. Put the dates in order, from shortest time to longest time between moonrise and moonset.

   _____

 Notes for Home: Your child used a table to calculate elapsed time.
Home Activity: Study the table with your child. Decide if the Moon can only be found in the sky at night or both at night and during daylight hours.

Notes

Dear Family,

Your child is learning about the different ways Earth and the Moon move. In the science chapter Patterns in the Sky, our class learned about Earth's rotation and its revolution around the Sun. Students also learned why the Moon appears to change shape throughout the month.

In addition to learning about Earth's movement and how it affects the seasons, students have also learned many new vocabulary words. Help your child to make these words a part of his or her own vocabulary by using them when you talk together about Earth's cycles.

> star
> axis
> rotation
> revolution
> phase
> lunar eclipse
> telescope
> constellation

The following pages include activities that you and your child can do together. By participating in your child's education, you will help to bring the learning home.

Family Science Activity
Sunrise/Sunset Patterns

Materials:
- paper
- pen or pencil
- newspaper (optional)

Steps

1. Choose to record the time the Sun rises in the morning, or the time the Sun sets in the evening, or both. This depends on the season and your schedule.

2. Help your child make a chart. Divide the chart into two columns. Entitle one column *Date*, the other column *Time*.

3. Every day for the next couple of weeks, invite your child to go outside and watch the Sun rise or set. He or she should record the date and time when the first or last rays of the Sun are visible. (You may wish to compare these times with official sunrise and sunset times on the weather page of the newspaper.)

4. After two weeks, look at the chart. Ask your child to explain the pattern he or she has recorded. Are the daylight hours getting longer or shorter? Why? How will the number of daylight hours change during the next season?

Phases of the Moon

Look at the pictures of the Moon below.

Draw lines to match the pictures on the left with the phase of the Moon on the right.

New Moon

Full Moon

First Quarter

Crescent

Your Favorite Season

Draw the weather for your favorite season.

Write about your favorite season. What is the temperature like? How much sunlight do you get each day?

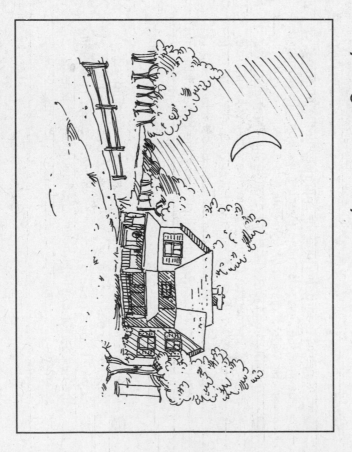

Match each vocabulary term with its meaning. Write the letter on the blank beside it.

____ 1. planet

a. to travel in an oval path

____ 2. asteroid

b. a body of matter that orbits the Sun

____ 3. orbit

c. the Sun, the nine planets, and their moons

____ 4. solar system

d. a chunk of rock in orbit around the Sun

In the box below, draw a picture to illustrate the vocabulary terms. Use the words as labels.

Notes for Home: Your child learned the vocabulary terms for Chapter 16.
Home Activity: Ask your child to use the drawing above to explain the meanings of the vocabulary terms. Talk about how planets move in the solar system.

Compare and Contrast

Read the science article. Use the information to compare and contrast Mercury and Pluto.

Mercury and Pluto

Mercury and Pluto are the two smallest planets in our solar system. Both are rocky. Mercury has no atmosphere, and Pluto has almost none. But in many ways, they are different. Mercury is closest to the Sun, so it is very dry and hot. Because Pluto is farthest from the Sun, it is very cold. Mercury orbits the Sun in just 88 Earth days, but Pluto takes 248 Earth years to travel around the Sun!

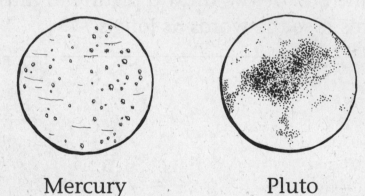

Mercury   Pluto

Apply It!

In the graphic organizer on the next page, write ways the two planets are alike in the middle section. Write ways they are different on the left and the right.

Characteristics of Mercury   **Both Mercury and Pluto**   **Characteristics of Pluto**

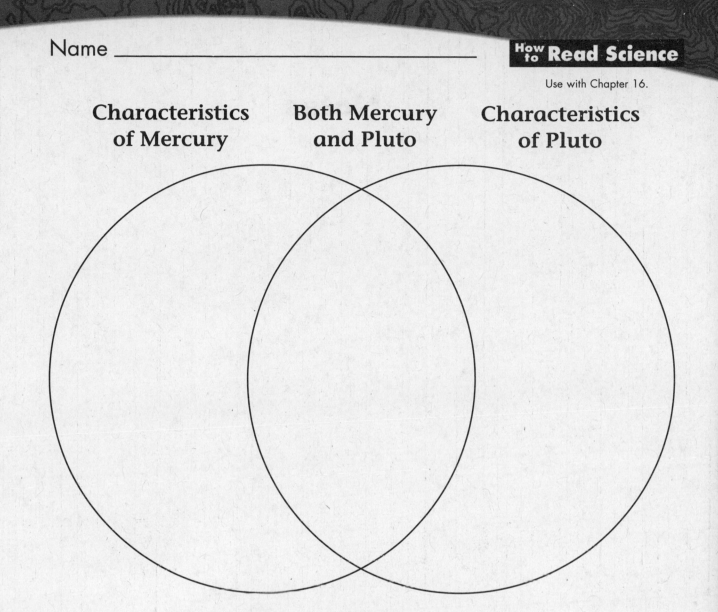

Notes for Home: Your child learned how to use a diagram to show how two subjects are different and alike.

Home Activity: Work with your child to make a list of ways the Moon and the Sun are alike and different.

Notes

Lesson 1: What are the parts of the solar system?

Before You Read Lesson 1

Read each statement below. Place a check mark in the circle to indicate whether you agree or disagree with the statement.

	Agree	Disagree
1. The Sun is the biggest, hottest star.	○	○
2. Nine planets make up the solar system.	○	○
3. Gravity makes planets orbit the Sun.	○	○

After You Read Lesson 1

Reread each statement above. If the lesson supports your choice, place a check mark in the *Correct* circle. Then explain how the text supports your choice. If the lesson does not support your choice, place a check mark in the *Incorrect* circle. Then explain why your choice is wrong.

	Correct	Incorrect
1. _____	○	○
_____		
2. _____	○	○
_____		
3. _____	○	○
_____		

Notes for Home: Your child has completed a pre/post inventory of key concepts in the lesson.
Home Activity: Ask your child to model the revolution and rotation of one of the planets in the solar system using a large ball and a small ball.

Reviewing Terms: Sentence Completion

Complete each sentence with the correct word or phrase.

_____ 1. A(n) _____ is a large body that revolves around the Sun. (planet, asteroid)

_____ 2. The Sun, nine planets, their moons, and other objects in orbit around the Sun make up _____. (the solar system, space)

_____ 3. An object's _____ is the path it takes around the Sun. (asteroid, orbit)

_____ 4. Chunks of rock that orbit the Sun are called _____. (asteroids, outer planets)

Reviewing Concepts: Sentence Completion

Complete each sentence with the correct word.

_____ 5. The Sun is a _____. (planet, star)

_____ 6. Planets are held in orbit by the Sun's _____. (gravity, plasma)

_____ 7. Mercury, Venus, Earth, and Mars are the _____ planets. (inner, outer)

_____ 8. The planets are divided into inner and outer planets based on their distance from the _____. (Moon, Sun)

Applying Strategies: Compare and Contrast

Use complete sentences to answer question 9. (2 points)

9. Name one way in which the Sun and the planets are similar. Name one way in which they are different.

_____

_____

_____

Lesson 2: What are the planets?

Before You Read Lesson 2

Read each statement below. Place a check mark in the circle to indicate whether you agree or disagree with the statement.

	Agree	Disagree
1. Mercury rotates slower than Earth.	◯	◯
2. Earth's atmosphere is important to life.	◯	◯
3. Jupiter and Pluto are gas giants.	◯	◯

After You Read Lesson 2

Reread each statement above. If the lesson supports your choice, place a check mark in the *Correct* circle. Then explain how the text supports your choice. If the lesson does not support your choice, place a check mark in the *Incorrect* circle. Then explain why your choice is wrong.

	Correct	Incorrect
1. _____	◯	◯
_____		
2. _____	◯	◯
_____		
3. _____	◯	◯
_____		

Notes for Home: Your child has completed a pre/post inventory of key concepts in the lesson.
Home Activity: Make flash cards with the names of the planets. Have your child place them in order from closest to farthest from the Sun and tell about each one.

Reviewing Concepts: True or False

Write **T** (True) or **F** (False) on the line before each statement.

_____ 1. The inner planets are gas giants.

_____ 2. Earth is the third planet from the Sun.

_____ 3. Mars is called the "red planet."

_____ 4. Earth can support life because of its temperature, atmosphere, and liquid water.

_____ 5. Earth's surface always stays the same.

_____ 6. The outer planets are much closer together than the inner planets.

_____ 7. Gas giants have rings around them.

_____ 8. Pluto is the smallest planet in the solar system.

Applying Strategies: Calculating

9. The distance across Earth is 12,750 kilometers. The distance across Venus is 12,000 kilometers. How much greater is the distance across Earth than the distance across Venus? Show your work. (2 points)

Finding Patterns in Tables

Every planet rotates. Some planets rotate faster than Earth, and some rotate slower than Earth. Look at the information in the table. The numbers show how many times each planet rotates for every one rotation of Earth.

Planets		Revolution Time (Earth Days)
Inner Planets	Mercury	58.8
	Venus	244
	Earth	1.0
	Mars	1.029
Outer Planets	Jupiter	0.411
	Saturn	0.428
	Uranus	0.748
	Neptune	0.802
	Pluto	0.267

1. How long does it take Venus to spin once on its axis?

   _____

2. Which planet rotates fastest?

   _____

3. How do the inner planets compare to the outer planets in rotation?

   _____

Notes for Home: Your child looked for patterns in a table.
Home Activity: With your child, search for an encyclopedia or magazine article on the solar system. Find a table comparing the planets in some way and look for a pattern.

Notes

Dear Family,

Your child is learning about the Sun, Earth, and the rest of the solar system. In the science chapter The Solar System, our class learned what the Sun is and how it makes heat and light. Students also found out how the planets move in space.

As students studied the characteristics of each planet, they also learned many new vocabulary words. Help your child to make these words a part of his or her own vocabulary by using them when you talk together about the solar system.

planet
solar system
orbit
asteroid

The following pages include activities that you and your child can do together. By participating in your child's education, you will help to bring the learning home.

© Pearson Education, Inc.

Family Science Activity
Solar System Demonstration

Materials:

- large round ball (for example: a basketball or soccer ball)
- smaller round ball (for example: a tennis ball or rubber ball)

Steps

1. Place both balls near one another on a countertop. Explain to your child that the larger ball is the Sun and the smaller ball is Earth.

2. Explain that the part of Earth facing the Sun is experiencing daytime. The part of Earth not facing the Sun is experiencing nighttime.

3. Have your child turn Earth in a complete circle. How many hours does it take for Earth to make one complete rotation? (24 hours)

4. Now have your child move Earth around the Sun. How many days does it take for Earth to make one complete orbit, or circle? (365 days)

Workbook

Space Detective

Circle the words in the puzzle below.

Y	X	I	L	N	Z	E	O	T	V	M	K
C	A	P	S	A	P	L	A	N	E	T	O
B	A	I	W	O	O	S	A	T	Y	P	I
A	S	A	T	M	O	S	P	H	E	R	E
S	A	Q	I	J	Y	S	E	I	O	N	Z
O	S	P	B	R	S	E	A	O	U	P	G
U	T	L	O	R	B	I	T	U	O	M	R
E	E	R	A	T	A	H	R	S	Y	O	A
P	R	L	M	U	I	R	P	T	R	V	P
R	O	D	U	O	I	D	T	A	E	T	I
S	I	D	P	L	A	M	T	E	A	T	I
U	D	Y	S	Y	R	E	V	O	L	V	Y

Word Bank

atmosphere	gravity	solar system
orbit	asteroid	
	planet	
	rotate	revolve

Planet Position

Write the names of the planets in their order from the Sun.

M _ _ _ _ _ _
V _ _ _ _ _
E _ _ _ _
M _ _ _
J _ _ _ _ _ _ _
S _ _ _ _ _
U _ _ _ _ _
N _ _ _ _ _ _ _
P _ _ _ _

Fun Fact

Use the word moon in many phrases. "To shoot for the moon" means to do something unusual. "Once in a blue moon" means very rarely. "Crying for the moon" means wanting something that is hard to get.

Match each vocabulary term with its meaning. Write the letter on the blank beside the word.

____ 1. technology

____ 2. invention

____ 3. tool

____ 4. computer

a. something made for the first time

b. machine for storing, processing, and getting information

c. device made by people to do work more easily

d. using knowledge to make tools and new ways to do things

Use each of the vocabulary terms from above to complete the diagram. Write the word that fits in the blank in each sentence.

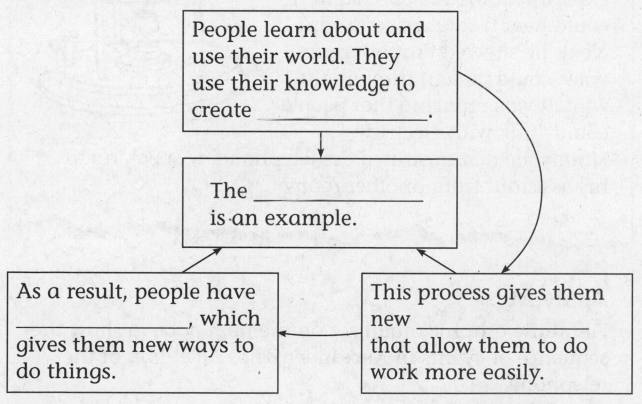

People learn about and use their world. They use their knowledge to create _____.

The _____ is an example.

As a result, people have _____, which gives them new ways to do things.

This process gives them new _____ that allow them to do work more easily.

Notes for Home: Your child learned the vocabulary terms for Chapter 17.
Home Activity: With your child, list some **tools** that make work easier, **inventions** that have changed our lives, and ways we use **technology** today.

Name _____

Sequence

Read the science article.

Telegraph Wire

Alexander Graham Bell knew a lot about sound and music. He wondered whether more than one message could be sent over a telegraph wire. First, he experimented to try to send signals with different pitch over one wire. Then, during his experiments, he discovered he could hear a sound over a wire. Next, he showed that a human voice could be sent through the wire. It was amazing that people could "talk with electricity"! Finally, he demonstrated the telephone by speaking to his assistant from another room.

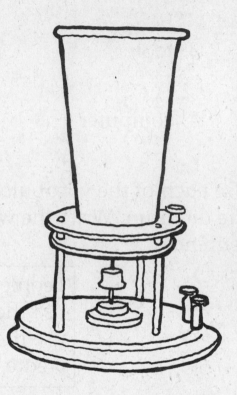

Apply It!

Fill in the graphic organizer on the next page to show the sequence of events in Alexander Bell's invention of the telephone.

© Pearson Education, Inc.

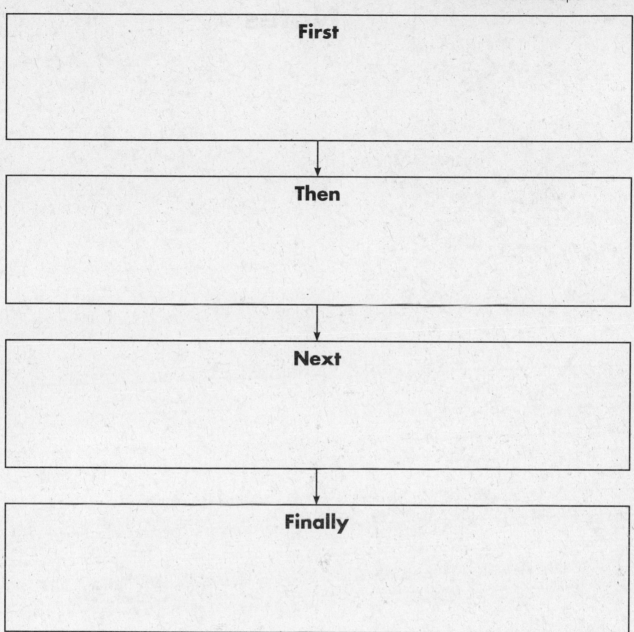

First

Then

Next

Finally

Notes for Home: Your child learned how to place events in logical, sequential order and use clue words signaling a sequence.
Home Activity: Ask your child to pick an electronic item he or she uses and explain the sequence of steps followed to use it.

Notes

Lesson 1: How does technology affect our lives?

Before You Read Lesson 1

Read each statement below. Place a check mark in the circle to indicate whether you agree or disagree with the statement.

	Agree	Disagree
1. People have used technology since the 1800s.	O	O
2. Inventions improve technology.	O	O
3. Technology systems work together.	O	O

After You Read Lesson 1

Reread each statement above. If the lesson supports your choice, place a check mark in the *Correct* circle. Then explain how the text supports your choice. If the lesson does not support your choice, place a check mark in the *Incorrect* circle. Then explain why your choice is wrong.

	Correct	Incorrect
1. _____ _____	O	O
2. _____ _____	O	O
3. _____ _____	O	O

Notes for Home: Your child has completed a pre/post inventory of key concepts in the lesson.
Home Activity: With your child, brainstorm a list of inventions that make your lives easier and more pleasant. Talk about how and why each might have been invented.

Name _____

Reviewing Terms: Matching

Match each description with the correct word. Write the letter on the line next to each description.

_____ 1. something that helps people do work more easily

_____ 2. the use of knowledge to design new tools and ways of doing things

_____ 3. something made for the first time

a. invention
b. tool
c. technology

Reviewing Concepts: True or False

Write **T** (True) or **F** (False) on the line before each statement.

_____ 4. People use technology to solve problems.

_____ 5. Technology was not used before the year 2000.

_____ 6. The systems in a house work together.

_____ 7. Ice boxes and refrigerators are both technology.

_____ 8. Technology will continue to change in the future.

Writing

Use complete sentences to answer question 9. (2 points)

9. Write one or two sentences that describe an invention you have used today.

_____

_____

_____

Lesson 2: What are some new technologies?

Before You Read Lesson 2

Read each statement below. Place a check mark in the circle to indicate whether you agree or disagree with the statement.

	Agree	Disagree
1. GPS uses a computer to figure out location.	○	○
2. Optical fibers improve communication.	○	○
3. TV was invented accidentally.	○	○

After You Read Lesson 2

Reread each statement above. If the lesson supports your choice, place a check mark in the *Correct* circle. Then explain how the text supports your choice. If the lesson does not support your choice, place a check mark in the *Incorrect* circle. Then explain why your choice is wrong.

	Correct	Incorrect
1. _____	○	○
_____		
2. _____	○	○
_____		
3. _____	○	○
_____		

Notes for Home: Your child has completed a pre/post inventory of key concepts in the lesson.
Home Activity: Ask your child to choose a technology discussed in the lesson and tell why he or she thinks it is important.

Reviewing Terms: Sentence Completion
Complete the sentence with the correct word.

_____ 1. A _____ is a machine that stores, processes, and sends electronic information. (microwave, computer)

Reviewing Concepts: Sentence Completion
Complete each sentence with the correct word or phrase.

_____ 2. A _____ helps navigators find their location. (GPS, microwave)

_____ 3. Calculators, cameras, and digital watches all use _____. (computer chips, satellites)

_____ 4. Optical fibers are made of _____. (copper, glass)

_____ 5. The first transportation system used in the United States was _____. (highways, rivers)

_____ 6. _____ are the fastest way to carry cargo from one place to another. (Planes, Trains)

_____ 7. Microwaves are a form of _____. (radiation, radar)

_____ 8. _____ is a technology that allows TV screens to be large and flat. (LCD, Glass)

Applying Strategies: Math
9. There are about one million trucks in the United States today. Write the number *one million* in standard notation. (2 points)

_____

Lesson 3: How does technology help us get energy?

Before You Read Lesson 3

Read each statement below. Place a check mark in the circle to indicate whether you agree or disagree with the statement.

	Agree	Disagree
1. Running water is needed to produce electricity.	○	○
2. Wind and water produce most of our power.	○	○
3. Houses can use solar power.	○	○

After You Read Lesson 3

Reread each statement above. If the lesson supports your choice, place a check mark in the *Correct* circle. Then explain how the text supports your choice. If the lesson does not support your choice, place a check mark in the *Incorrect* circle. Then explain why your choice is wrong.

	Correct	Incorrect
1. _____	○	○
_____		
2. _____	○	○
_____		
3. _____	○	○
_____		

Notes for Home: Your child has completed a pre/post inventory of key concepts in the lesson.
Home Activity: With your child, find out how the electricity you use is produced. Discuss some ways this method affects the environment.

Reviewing Concepts: True or False

Write **T** (True) or **F** (False) on the line before each statement.

_____ 1. Water was used for energy before electricity was invented.

_____ 2. Windmills and water-powered mills pollute the air and water.

_____ 3. Wind and water are renewable resources.

_____ 4. Hydroelectric power dams are used to make electricity.

_____ 5. The energy in burning coal can be used to make electricity.

_____ 6. Solar energy is the energy of wind.

_____ 7. Windmills change the kinetic energy of wind to electricity.

_____ 8. Through all of history, technology has been developed only in the United States.

Applying Strategies: Sequence

9. The steps of using coal to make electricity are shown below, but they are out of order. Use the clue words to write the steps in the correct order. (2 points)

Finally, pressure from steam turns wheels in electricity generators.
Next, heat is used to boil water.
First, coal is burned to produce heat.
Then boiling water makes steam.

_____

_____

_____

_____

Technology Time Line

In less than a hundred years, people went from the invention of the airplane to sending people into outer space. Look at the events listed in the chart. Mark each event on the time line below, then label it. The first item is done for you.

History of Flight

Year	Event
1903	First gas-powered, manned airplane flight
1926	First liquid-filled rocket launch
1958	First satellite orbits Earth
1969	First manned spacecraft lands on the Moon
1981	First flight of spacecraft that returns, lands, and can be reused
2000	First crew sent to International Space Station

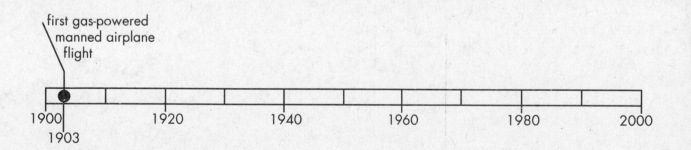

first gas-powered manned airplane flight

1900 1920 1940 1960 1980 2000
1903

Notes for Home: Your child recorded events on a time line.
Home Activity: Help your child make a table showing important events in his or her life and the date they occurred. Then have your child transfer them to a time line like the one shown on this page.

© Pearson Education, Inc.

Notes

Dear Family,

Your child is learning about how science and technology can affect our daily lives. In the chapter Science in Our Lives, our class has learned about how technology helps us solve problems. We have also learned about new technologies, such as Global Positioning Systems (GPS), and how they improve our lives.

Students have also learned many new vocabulary words. Help your child make these words a part of his or her own vocabulary by using them when you talk together about science and technological advances.

tool
technology
invention
computer

The following pages include activities that you and your child can do together. By participating in your child's education, you will help to bring the learning home.

© Pearson Education, Inc.

Family Science Activity
Technology Collage

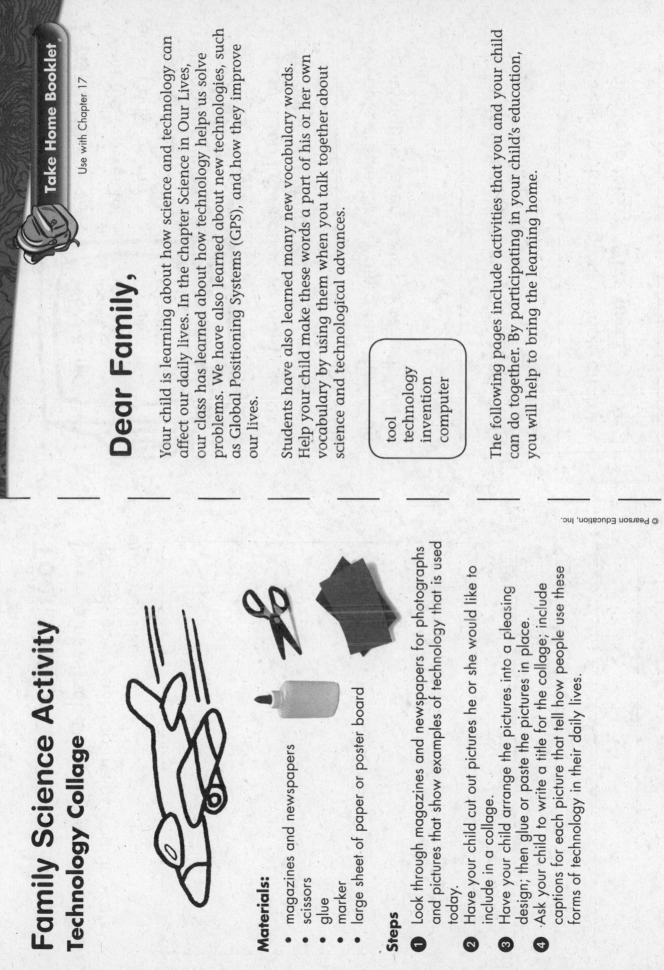

Materials:

- magazines and newspapers
- scissors
- glue
- marker
- large sheet of paper or poster board

Steps

1. Look through magazines and newspapers for photographs and pictures that show examples of technology that is used today.

2. Have your child cut out pictures he or she would like to include in a collage.

3. Have your child arrange the pictures into a pleasing design; then glue or paste the pictures in place.

4. Ask your child to write a title for the collage; include captions for each picture that tell how people use these forms of technology in their daily lives.

Vocabulary Practice

Write the answer for each riddle on the line. Each answer is a vocabulary word.

Word Bank
tool
technology
invention
computer

1. I can keep information so that you don't forget it. What am I?

_____

2. People created me. I am a telephone, an automobile, even a simple wheel. What am I?

_____

3. I am something you use to do work more easily. What am I?

_____

4. You use me to design new tools and new ways to do things. What am I?

_____

Tool Time

Invent a new tool. Draw it. Write sentences that tell how your tool helps you do work more easily.

_____

_____

_____

Name _____

What is the life cycle of a plant?

Growing plants need water, air, the right temperature, and sunlight. The pictures below show the life cycle of a peanut plant.

2. The seed grows a **stem** and a **root**.

1. The part of a peanut you eat is a **seed**.

3. The peanut plant grows leaves. It can start making sugar for food.

4. The **adult plant** makes seeds underground.

Answer the questions.

1. How many steps are there in the life cycle of a peanut?

_____

2. What can a peanut plant do when it grows leaves?

_____

3. Where does an adult peanut plant make its seeds?

_____

4. What does a growing plant need?

_____

How is a flower pollinated?

Bees, other animals, or wind pollinate a flower. This happens when they move pollen to the part of the flower that makes seeds. After a flower is pollinated, it grows seeds and fruit.

A flower's colorful petals may attract bees and other animals to the flower.

This bee is looking for food. It has pollen on its body. The bee moves pollen to the part of the flower that makes seeds.

Pollen put on the tip of this part helps form seeds here.

This part of the flower makes the pollen.

Answer these questions.

1. Why is the bee coming to the flower?

   _____

2. What part of the flower attracts animals?

   _____

3. What part of the plant makes seeds?

   _____

4. How do bees, wind, and other animals pollinate a plant?

   _____

5. What happens after a flower is pollinated?

   _____

Name _____

What are invertebrates?

Invertebrates do not have backbones. Invertebrates are the largest group of animals on Earth.

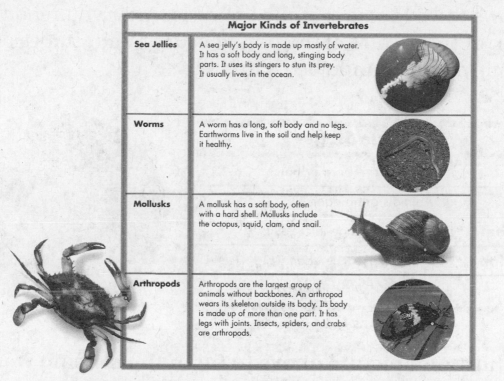

Major Kinds of Invertebrates

Sea Jellies	A sea jelly's body is made up mostly of water. It has a soft body and long, stinging body parts. It uses its stingers to stun its prey. It usually lives in the ocean.
Worms	A worm has a long, soft body and no legs. Earthworms live in the soil and help keep it healthy.
Mollusks	A mollusk has a soft body, often with a hard shell. Mollusks include the octopus, squid, clam, and snail.
Arthropods	Arthropods are the largest group of animals without backbones. An arthropod wears its skeleton outside its body. Its body is made up of more than one part. It has legs with joints. Insects, spiders, and crabs are arthropods.

Answer the following questions.

1. What do all invertebrates have in common?

_____

2. What kind of invertebrate is an octopus?

_____

3. What do sea jellies, worms, and mollusks have in common?

_____

4. What kind of invertebrate is a fly?

_____

5. Which is the largest group of animals on Earth?

_____

How do animals grow and change?

All animals grow and change during their life cycle. The chart below shows the five stages of the life cycle. After you read the chart, look at the picture of the panda bears. What stages of the life cycle are the panda bears in?

Life Cycle Stages	
Birth	Animals are born or hatch.
Growth	Animals get bigger.
Development	Animals change into adults.
Reproduction	Animals produce young.
Death	Animals' lives come to an end.

Use the chart and picture above to fill in the missing words below.

1. The panda bear cub is in the (reproduction/birth)

   _____ stage of life.

2. The mother panda bear is in the (reproduction/

   development) _____ stage of life.

3. The _____ stage of life is when an animal changes into an adult.

4. Animals get bigger during the _____ stage.

5. Animals' lives come to an end at _____.

What is in an ecosystem?

The environment of a living thing is everything that surrounds it. An ecosystem is all the living and nonliving things that interact with each other in an environment. Climate shapes each environment. Climate is the weather in a place all year.

A Desert Ecosystem.
The Joshua Tree National Park is a desert ecosystem. The desert gets very little rain. It is hot during the day and cool at night. At night, the bobcat hunts for birds and other small animals. The sidewinder rattlesnake usually hunts at night for small animals to eat.

Answer these questions about the ecosystem above.

1. What is the climate like? Is it hot or cold? Wet or dry?

   _____

2. What living things do you see?

   _____

3. Is this ecosystem a good place for a bobcat? Why?

   _____

4. Why do you think the rattlesnake hunts at night?

Name _____

How do ecosystems change over time?

Ecosystems begin to change when one part of the ecosystem changes. For example, if it rains more than usual, plants grow more. Then, squirrels have more food to eat. The squirrel population grows. Coyotes eat squirrels. When there are more squirrels to eat, the coyote population begins to grow.

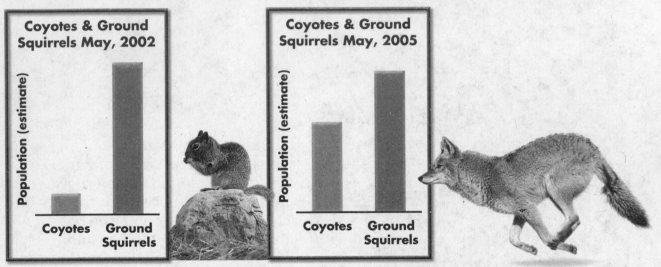

If there is more food, the squirrel population grows.

A larger squirrel population means more food for coyotes. The coyote population grows.

Answer these questions about the information above.

1. How can weather help change an ecosystem?

_____

2. What happens to the squirrel population when there are more plants?

_____

_____

3. Why does the coyote population grow?

_____

Name _____

How do living things get energy?

Sunlight provides the energy for plants. Plants make their own food with energy from the Sun. They are producers. Animals get their energy from plants or from eating other animals. They are consumers.

A Food Chain

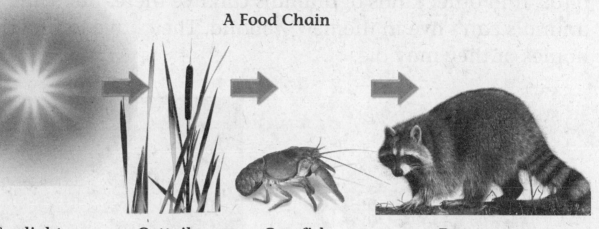

Sunlight   Cattails   Crayfish   Raccoon

Answer these questions about the food chain above.

1. Where does the energy begin in this food chain?

_____

2. Who are the producers in this food chain?

_____

3. Who are the consumers in this food chain?

_____

4. Do you think the raccoon is the end of this food chain? Explain.

_____

_____

© Pearson Education, Inc.

Name _____

How do beavers change the environment?

Plants and animals can change their environment. For example, beavers build dams of sticks and mud. Water backs up behind the dam and a new wetland habitat grows. Fish, birds, and other kinds of animals can live there. But some animals can't live in the new wetland. They have to find new homes or they may die.

Beaver

Beaver dam

Answer these questions.

1. How do beavers change their environments?

_____

2. What kind of new habitat grows around a beaver dam?

_____

3. What kinds of animals can now live in the wetland habitat?

_____

4. What happens to animals who can't live in the new wetland?

_____

Name _____

Where do people get fresh water?

People need to drink fresh water. Only a small amount of the water on Earth is fresh water. Most fresh water is frozen as ice. Some fresh water comes from underground. This is called groundwater. A spring is a stream of groundwater that flows from underground. People also dig wells to get groundwater. We also get fresh water from lakes, rivers, and streams.

Most fresh water is frozen as ice. This iceberg is near Antarctica.

A spring is a stream of groundwater.

Answer these questions about fresh water.

1. Why do people need fresh water?

_____

2. In what form is most of the fresh water on Earth?

_____

3. Some fresh water flows from underground. What is this called?

_____

4. What are some other ways people get fresh water?

_____

_____

Name _____

How does water move around Earth?

The water cycle is the movement of water from Earth's surface into the air and back again. Water changes during the water cycle. The Sun and wind cause water to evaporate and water to change into water vapor. Water vapor rises into cooler air and changes into water droplets. This is called condensation. When water droplets get too heavy, they fall to Earth as rain, snow, sleet, or hail.

Precipitation

Evaporation

Groundwater flow

Stream water flow

Answer these questions about the water cycle.

1. The picture shows water moving from Earth's surface to the air and back again. What is this called?

_____

2. What does water change into when it evaporates?

_____

3. What does water vapor change into when it rises?

_____

4. When water droplets get heavy, what happens?

_____

© Pearson Education, Inc.

Workbook

How can scientists measure weather?

Scientists use many tools to measure and describe weather, and help describe the atmosphere. The atmosphere has weight, so it presses down with a force called air pressure. Low air pressure often means weather will be cloudy or rainy. High air pressure often means clear skies.

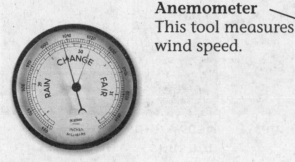

Anemometer
This tool measures
wind speed.

Wind Vane
This tool records the
direction of the wind.

Barometer
This tool measures
air pressure.

Answer these questions about measuring weather.

1. Which tool measures wind speed?

   _____

2. What is a wind vane used for?

   _____

3. What are all of these tools used for?

   _____

4. What causes air pressure?

   _____

5. If the air pressure is low, how will the weather probably be?

   _____

Name _____

What are some dangerous storms?

Some storms can be dangerous. **Hurricanes** are huge storms that form over the ocean. Hurricanes have heavy rains, winds, and waves. **Tornadoes** are spinning columns of air that form beneath thunderstorm clouds. Tornadoes are much smaller than hurricanes, but can have stronger winds. A **blizzard** is a winter snow storm.

Hurricanes do the most damage when they move over land.

A **blizzard** is a winter storm with low temperatures and blowing snow.

Heavy rains and high waves can cause floods.

Most **tornadoes** have very strong winds.

Answer these questions.

1. When do hurricanes cause the most damage?

   _____

2. What is a blizzard?

   _____

3. What causes floods?

   _____

4. How are tornadoes and hurricanes alike? Different?

   _____

   _____

   _____

   _____

What are the three main rock groups?

There are three main groups of rocks: **igneous**, **sedimentary**, and **metamorphic**. Each group contains many kinds of rocks.

Igneous

Sedimentary

Metamorphic

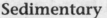

This granite is igneous rock. All igneous rock has grains. The grains can be large or small.

This shale is sedimentary rock. All sedimentary rock has layers.

This gneiss was once igneous rock with grains. The grains of gneiss are now layers. All metamorphic rocks changed from another kind of rock.

This slate was once sedimentary rock. The slate doesn't have layers like shale.

Answer these questions about rock groups.

1. What is an example of an igneous rock?

   _____

2. What is an example of a sedimentary rock?

   _____

3. In what way is a metamorphic rock different from the other groups?

   _____

4. What kind of rock is shale? What can shale turn into?

   _____

5. What kind of rock does gneiss come from?

   _____

What are some properties of minerals?

A **mineral** is a natural material that forms from nonliving matter. Rocks are made up of minerals. You can compare minerals by **color**, **luster** (the way they reflect light), **streak** (the kind of mark they make), and **hardness**.

Properties of Minerals

Mineral		Color	Luster	Streak	Hardness
Mica This mineral breaks into flaky pieces when it is struck.		black, gray, green, violet	pearly on surfaces	white	can be scratched with a knife
Molybdenite This is one of the strongest minerals and is used very often. It resiststs heat.		silvery	metallic	bluish gray	can be scratched with a fingernail
Crocoite This mineral is often found in Australia.		reddish-orange	very shiny	orange-yellow	can be scratched with a coin

Answer these questions.

1. Which mineral is the softest? How do you know?

   _____

   _____

2. Which mineral would sparkle less in the sunshine? Why?

   _____

3. What happens if you scratch Molybdenite against another rock?

   _____

4. Which of the minerals would be safest to use near fires?

What is weathering?

Any action that breaks rocks into smaller pieces is called **weathering**. There are many reasons why weathering happens. Freezing and thawing of water can break up rocks. Plants and animals can also cause weathering.

Weathering
As the roots in this tree grow,
they help to break up rock.

Answer these questions about weathering.

1. What is weathering?

_____

2. What are some of the reasons for weathering?

_____

3. How are the tree roots changing the rock?

_____

4. What kind of landform does this picture show?

What is erosion?

After weathering happens, the materials can stay in place or move. When weathered material such as rock or sand moves, **erosion** takes place. Wind, water, glaciers, and gravity can cause erosion.

This is Bryce Canyon in Utah. Rain and melting snow caused erosion. The strange shapes are called "hoodoos."

Answer the following questions.

1. What caused erosion in this picture?

   _____

2. What forces can cause erosion?

   _____

3. What are the strange shapes in Bryce Canyon called?

   _____

Name _____

What is conservation?

Some natural resources can be used up. Others can be used again and again. It's important that we protect our natural resources. When we do not waste or use up a natural resource, we practice **conservation**.

Water from homes is filtered through sand in ponds like these. Farmers use the recycled water for their orange trees.

Dirty water is piped into a wetland in Florida. It will become clean enough to be piped back into a river.

Answer these questions about conservation.

1. What natural resource do you see in both photographs?

    _____

2. How is conservation practiced in the wetlands?

    _____

3. How is water recycled for the trees in the photo on the right?

    _____

4. What are some ways you can help with water conservation?

    _____

How much is a year of trash?

A landfill is an area where trash is buried. The trash in a landfill never goes away. So, more and more area is needed for landfills.

What is in a Year's Worth of My Trash?	
Materials	**Mass (in kilograms)**
Paper	250
Plastic	80
Metal (steel cans)	40
Metal (aluminum cans)	10
Glass	40
Food scraps	80

Answer these questions.

1. What kind of trash do people throw away the most?

_____

2. How much plastic and glass do people usually throw away in a year?

_____

3. How can you help with paper conservation?

_____

Name _____

How do we measure volume?

The **volume** of an object is the amount of space it takes up. You can measure the volume of solid objects. The unit of measure for volume is the **cube unit**. To find the volume of a solid object, you measure how many cube units fit into it.

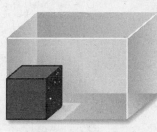

1 cubic unit

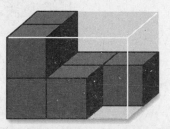

Fill the box with cubes to find its volume.

Answer these questions about measuring volume.

1. What is a cubic unit used for?

   _____

2. How is the volume of the box above measured?

   _____

3. What could you measure with cubic units in your classroom?

   _____

   _____

How do we measure volume?

We use the **cube unit** to measure volume.

12 cubes fill the box.
The volume is
12 cubic units.

Answer these questions.

1. How many cubes fill the box?

   _____

2. How do you know the volume of a box?

   _____

3. Is there another way you could measure the volume of the box?

   _____

   _____

What are the three states of matter?

Matter can be in three different forms: solid, liquid, and gas. Physical changes such as changing the temperature, causes matter to change states. When matter changes from one state to another, it remains the same kind of matter.

States of Water

Ice is a **solid** and the particles are close together.

In **liquid** water, water particles slide past one another.

The water particles are far apart in the **gas** called water vapor.

Answer these questions about matter.

1. What is the same about the matter in the 3 containers?

   _____

2. What are the 3 different states of matter in the pictures?

   _____

3. What causes water to change form?

   _____

Name _____

What is a chemical change?

In a chemical change, one kind of matter changes into another but usually cannot be changed back.

Rusting is a slow chemical change. Helped by water, the iron chain combines with oxygen gas in the air and slowly changes to rust. The rust cannot change back into iron.

Burning is a fast chemical change. When the sticks burn, the wood changes to gases and ashes. The sticks are no longer wood.

Answer these questions.

1. What do the picures both show?

_____

2. Which material shows slow chemical change?

_____

3. Which material shows a fast chemical change?

_____

4. Can either the iron or the wood change back to the kind of matter they were at first?

_____

How does force affect motion?

A push or a pull makes an object move.

The teams are pulling the rope in opposite directions. The team that pulls the rope with greater force will move the rope in its direction.

Answer these questions about force and motion.

1. What happens if you push or pull an object?

_____

2. How are the teams in the picture acting in the same way?

_____

3. How are the teams acting differently from one another?

_____

4. Which team will win this tug-of-war?

_____

How do simple machines affect work?

Simple machines make it easier for people to do work. Inclined planes and wedges are two simple machines that help make work easier.

An inclined plane, or a **ramp**, is a slanting surface that connects a lower level to a higher level.

The axe head is a wedge. Wedges are used to split, cut, or fasten things.

Answer these questions.

1. What do simple machines do?

_____

2. What are two kinds of simple machines?

_____

3. What are wedges used for?

_____

4. What is an inclined plane?

_____

_____

How does energy change form?

Energy comes in different forms. Here are five forms of energy you use every day.

Forms of Energy

Chemical	Kinetic	Electrical	Light	Thermal
		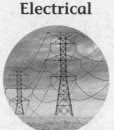		
This energy holds particles of matter together, especially in food.	This is the energy of moving objects. Moving parts in playground equipment use this energy.	This energy can pass through special wires. We use this energy to power appliances.	The Sun's rays are light energy. Plants make food with light energy.	We feel this energy as heat.

Answer these questions.

1. Which kind of energy does a seesaw at a playground use?

   _____

2. Which kind of energy does a plant use to make food?

   _____

3. Which kind of energy does a fire produce?

   _____

4. Which kind of energy does a computer need to run?

   _____

What is electrical energy?

Follow the path of the electric energy from one place to another.

1. Electric current flows along a path from the negative part of the battery.

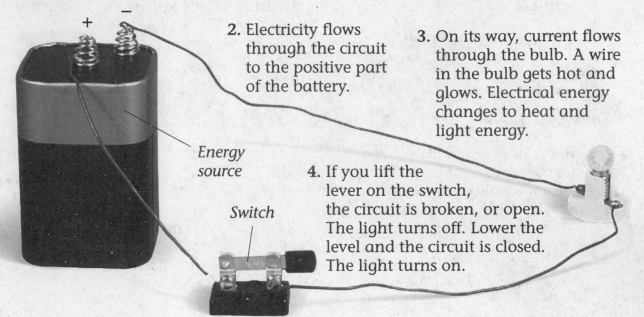

2. Electricity flows through the circuit to the positive part of the battery.

3. On its way, current flows through the bulb. A wire in the bulb gets hot and glows. Electrical energy changes to heat and light energy.

Energy source

Switch

4. If you lift the lever on the switch, the circuit is broken, or open. The light turns off. Lower the level and the circuit is closed. The light turns on.

Answer these questions.

1. From where does electric current flow?

_____

2. How does electrical energy change the bulb?

_____

_____

3. What happens if you lift the switch?

_____

4. What would happen if you lower the lever?

_____

Name _____

What are vocal cords?

You are able to speak and sing because your vocal cords vibrate, or move back and forth. When you speak, your vocal cords tighten. They vibrate as air passes between them. Tight vocal cords make the pitch of your voice higher. Loose vocal cords make the pitch of your voice lower.

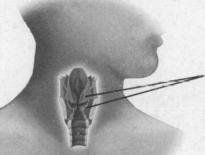

Vocal cords are the two pairs of thin tissue in the windpipe.

Answer these questions about vocal cords.

1. What are vocal cords?

   _____

2. Where are your vocal cords?

   _____

3. Place your fingers across your vocal cords. Hum lightly. What happens?

   _____

   _____

4. What happens to the pitch of your voice when your vocal cords tighten?

   _____

How do we hear?

Our ears receive sound waves that travel to our brain. The brain identifies the signals as sounds. This is how we hear.

The **outer ear** collects sound waves traveling in air.

The eardrum causes three **tiny bones** in the middle part of the ear to vibrate.

When sound waves hit the **eardrum**, it begins to vibrate.

The **inner ear** is also filled with liquid. Movement of tiny bones makes tiny hairs in the liquid vibrate. The hairs are attached to nerves that carry signals to the brain.

Answer these questions.

1. In what order do the parts of the ear work in order for you to hear?

   _____

2. What are the tiny hairs and liquid in the inner ear connected to?

   _____

3. What happens to the eardrum when sound waves hit it?

   _____

© Pearson Education, Inc.

What are some patterns that repeat every day?

Earth is always moving. Earth spins, or rotates, on its axis.
Earth makes one complete spin, or rotation, every 24 hours.
During this time, half of Earth always faces the Sun. That half
of Earth has day.

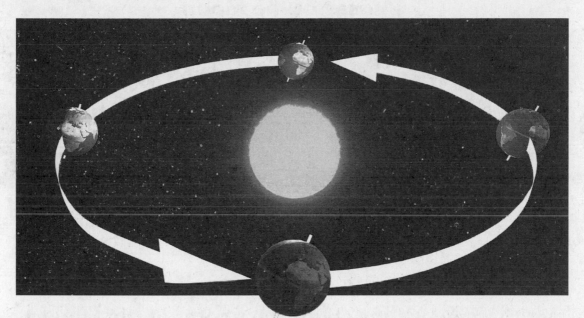

Earth makes one revolution every time it travels around the Sun. One
revolution takes one year.

Answer these questions about Earth's movement.

1. Describe the two ways in which Earth moves.

   _____

2. How long does it take for Earth to make one complete spin,
   or rotation?

   _____

3. How long does it take for Earth to make one revolution
   around the Sun?

   _____

Name _____

What are the phases of the Moon?

The drawing below shows the Moon circling Earth. Half of the Moon is always lighted by sunlight. The lighted half of the Moon cannot always be seen from Earth. Each different way the Moon can be seen from Earth is a phase of the Moon. The pattern of the phases of the Moon takes about four weeks.

Phases of the Moon

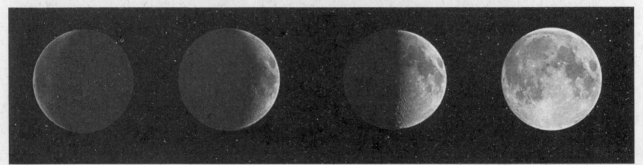

New Moon
We cannot see the Moon.

Crescent
We see only a small piece of the lighted part of the Moon.

First Quarter
The Moon looks like a half circle.

Full Moon
We can see all of the lighted part of the Moon.

Answer these questions about the phases of the Moon.

1. What is a phase of the Moon?

_____

2. What does the Moon look like during First Quarter?

_____

3. Why can't we see the Moon during the New Moon phase?

_____

_____

4. How much of the Moon do we see during the Crescent phase?

_____

Name _____

How do planets in our solar system move?

Earth is one of nine planets in our solar system. Earth and the other planets travel, or revolve, around the Sun, which is the center of the solar system. Each complete path around the Sun is an **orbit**. The strong pull of gravity keeps planets in their orbits.

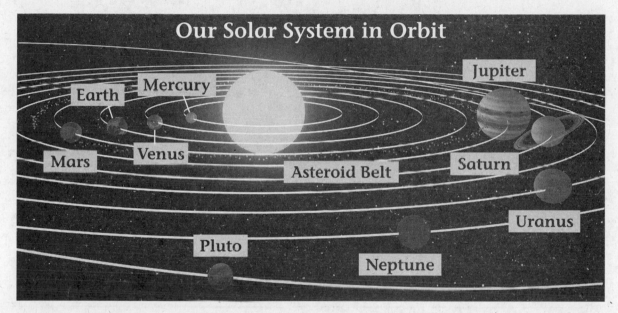

Our Solar System in Orbit

Answer these questions.

1. Which planet is closer to the Sun: Venus or Mars?

   _____

2. Which planet is further from Earth: Mercury or Pluto?

   _____

3. How is the Sun different from other planets?

   _____

   _____

4. What keeps the planets in orbit?

   _____

© Pearson Education, Inc.

Name _____

What is Earth?

From space, Earth is blue, white, and brown. Blue water covers three fourths of Earth's surface. Clouds and large caps of ice appear white. The land appears brown. Earth supports life because of its warm temperatures, water, and atmosphere.

The coldest place on Earth is Antarctica.

The hottest place in the United States is Death Valley, California. A very hot 57°C (134°F) has been recorded there.

Earth

Answer these questions.

1. What color is Antarctica in this photograph? Why?

   _____

2. What color is the hottest place in the United States? Why?

   _____

3. How would you know where to point to an ocean?

   _____

4. Will the cloud patterns swirling around Earth always look the same? Why not?

   _____

5. What would happen to life on Earth if there were no water?

   _____

Name _____

What are some technology systems in a house?

Parts of a house or apartment work together as a system that interacts.

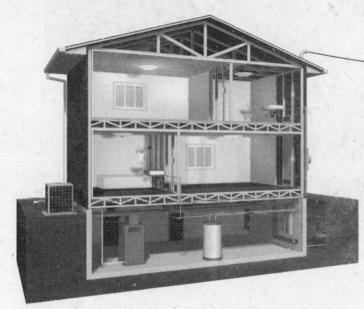

Technology in a Home

Systems in a House
Framing
Roofing and waterproofing
Electrical
Plumbing
Heating/cooling

Answer these questions.

1. What house system do walls and floors belong to?

   _____

2. What object in the diagram is part of the heating/cooling system?

   _____

   _____

3. Name some appliances that use technology from the electrical system in your house.

   _____

What is solar energy?

To meet our energy needs, people work hard to come up with new technologies and inventions. Solar energy is energy from sunlight. It does not cost very much.

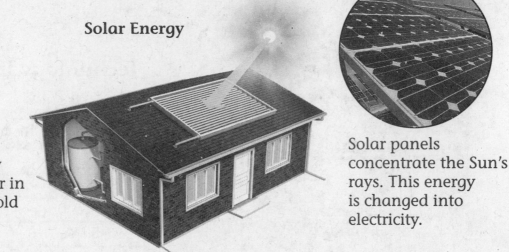

Solar Energy

Solar energy warms water in this household appliance.

Solar panels concentrate the Sun's rays. This energy is changed into electricity.

Answer these questions about solar energy.

1. Where do you find solar panels?

   _____

2. How do solar panels help turn lights on in a house?

   _____

   _____

3. How do solar panels help you take a hot bath or shower?

   _____

   _____

4. Why would it be hard to use solar panels for heat and electricity if you lived deep in woods?

   _____

   _____

Picture Credits

Illustration

176 Peter Bollinger
193, 194 Jeff Mangiat
195, 196, 197 Paul Oglesby
199, 200 Robert Ulrich

Photographs

Every effort has been made to secure permission and provide appropriate credit for photographic material. The publisher deeply regrets any omission and pledges to correct errors called to its attention in subsequent editions.

Unless otherwise acknowledged, all photographs are the property of Scott Foresman, a division of Pearson Education.

167 © DK Images, © Nigel Cattlin/Holt Studios, © Nigel Cattlin/Photo Researchers, Inc., © Kenneth W. Fink/Photo Researchers, Inc. 168 © DK Images, Getty Images. 169 © Charles Melton/Visuals Unlimited, © Brad Mogen/Visuals Unlimited, © Dick Scott/ Visuals Unlimited, © DK Images, © Bettmann/Corbis. 170 © Danny Lehman/Corbis, © Robert PIckett/Corbis, © The Image Bank/Getty Images, © Brian Rogers/Visuals Unlimited. 171 Daniel J. Cox/Natural Exposures, © J. Eastcott/Y. Eastcott Film/NGS Image Collection. 172 Darren Bennett/Animals Animals/Earth Scenes, © Joseph Van Os/Getty Images. 173 © Chase Swift/Corbis, © Carol Havens/Corbis, © Frank Blackburn; Ecoscene/ Corbis, © D. Robert and Lorri Franz/Corbis. 174 Photo Researchers, Inc., © Richard H. Johnston/Getty Images. 175 © M. Timothy O'Keefe/Bruce Coleman Inc., © Wolfgang Kaehler/Corbis. 177 © Terry Renna/AP/Wide World Photos, © Boden/Ledingham/Masterfile Corporation, Digital Vision, © Allan Davey/Masterfile Corporation. 178 © Leonard Lessin/ Peter Arnold, Inc., © DK Images. 179 © DK Images, © Andrew J. Martinez/Photo Researchers, Inc. 180 © DK Images. 181 © Fred Whitehead/Animals Animals/Earth Scenes. 182 © William Manning/Corbis. 183 © Alan Towse/Ecoscene/Corbis, © Kevin Fleming/ Corbis. 188 © Richard Megna/Fundamental Photographs, © DK Images. 189 © Rolf Bruderer/Corbis, © Bob Daemmrich/Corbis, © DK Images. 190 © AGStockUSA, Inc./Alamy Images, © Henry T. Kaiser/Index Stock Imagery, © Lester Lefkowitz/Corbis, © Mark L. Stephenson/Corbis, © Mark C. Burnett/Photo Researchers, Inc. 196 © John Sanford/Photo Researchers, Inc. 198 NOAA, © Maria Stenzel/NGS Image Collection, © Bill Varie/Corbis. 200 Getty Images

Notes